The Prayer Paradigm

A Strategic Way to Amplify Your Prayer Life

Julian Young

Published by Crown Media Publishing.
PO Box 4838
Omaha, NE 68104

Crown Media Publishing is committed to excellence in the publishing industry.

ISBN: 978-1502908063

Cover design by Forza Design
Interior design by Brittany Young

For information about bulk purchases of this book, please go to
www.julianyoung.co

Contents

To my wife Brittany and daughter Genesis.

Acknowledgements

To my brother Teddy, you have been there for me when all odds have stood against me. Secretly you've always been my hero. You have been an inspiration that is hard to describe. Thank you for not giving up on me, your faith, and most importantly yourself. Thank you for being a life changer.

Introduction: The Prayer Paradigm Shift

The mindset of prosperity is powered by true access to the value and meaning we possess as inherent creations designed in the likeness of the Creator. This paradigm of oneness with our Creator and the ability of having constant access to communion and fellowship with Him is all just a proverbial paradox of the supernatural without real tangible manifestations of our God-life influencing our everyday affairs.

Life in the Kingdom of God does not base itself on one-time happenings or what I like to call "experimental faith." On the contrary, the Kingdom comes to produce a tangible life experience that will become a standard and reference point of faith for future encounters with God.

This means there is a distinct difference between experimental faith and experienced faith. Faith that is experimental has no real personal evidence of what the law of faith can do for one's life. In the same token, when a person has a real tangible experience with faith it will become a milestone of expectation and the seed of an empowered belief system that God is truly unlimited and able to do anything.

If there is no constant momentum being built based on the evidence of consistent happenings, faith becomes an outer experience rather than a personal one. We began to view the Kingdom from an objective instead of a subjective experience, not really seeing how heaven can have an authentic impact in our lives and in present circumstances today. One of the greatest pitfalls that exist as a result of this objective mindset and approach to Kingdom living is the inability to see yourself doing what God says you can do. Believe it or not, nothing that God has promised you or said about you in His Word will have any real meaning to you unless you can see yourself doing it and possessing it.

But how do you create such a picture in your thoughts with so many images of disappointment and unfavorable outcomes lingering and constantly replaying themselves in the corridors of your mind? How do you overcome the frustration of unanswered prayer and supplication to rise to a level of a complete state of thinking? Whether you realize it or not, that psychological state of wholeness and perfection exists within your inner being. You have within your spirit the ability to connect to a God-life in you that is painting a clear picture of what you possess as a citizen, son, and royal heir to the Kingdom of God.

That life represents the authentic you. The original unlimited and unrestricted you within waiting to reclaim its rightful throne in the governing seat of your heart. You have to take back the Kingdom in you!

This is where true prosperity lies within the boundless confines of heaven's reality and supernatural life inside. Here your most compelling life exists; a life full of expectation and free from sorrowful living. A life of increase and blessing that produces perpetual breakthrough and overflow of God's favor and promises. Prayer has the ability to unleash this tangible life. Prayer is your connection point with the God-life that's inside you. When prayer is functioned properly, divine systems of communication become powerful entry points of heavenly invasions turning the tides of life into waves of increase and favor.

We have to be increasingly aware of the poverty mindset produced by lack of tangible Kingdom experience that causes us to constantly approach prayer from the defeated aspect of life. I would suggest that 90% of prayer has to do with the mindset and approach of the person.

THE PRAYER PARADIGM

An internal paradigm lens being shaped by the negative experiences of unanswered prayer will only continue to perpetuate negative images for your mind to feed on. Since confidence is a key factor in powerful effective praying, many people have already lost the battle that pertains to the mind, thus losing the battle of successful praying. Although prayer is not a battle, the struggle between faith and fear still is prevalent in the face of an expecting heart.

Poverty then infects the mind with hopelessness and doubt, producing the weight of insecurity. This becomes the platform of expression and birthing place of helpless, defeated praying. Have you ever noticed the tendency of most individuals praying is to always approach God with need? Why is it that many people always take the defensive end of praying as though we are losing and need God's help to win? My friends, this was never the intended state for the law of prayer. Jesus was clear in Matthew 6 that prayer is not designed for need.

We have to use the fresh wisdom and strategic revelation to move beyond the barrier of defeated-end praying. That battle is over and God is not on the losing end either; I can promise you that. This means as His royal heirship you are winning, and a beneficiary to that triumph.

Without this understanding of a winner's mindset and approach to prayer we will continue to pray defeated prayers asking and asking, fighting and fighting, continuing in a self-imposed cycle of needless war and exhaustion. When you tap into the Kingdom paradigm of praying, the force of God's will causes you to live above the gravitational pull of slavish fear and abandonment that cause you to feel incomplete and in need. The true state of a redeemed, born again Kingdom citizen is the realization of their complete state as flawless reflections of the Creator.

How then can we have a need? Need-based praying does not take root in God's Kingdom. It's a fallen paradigm or state of thinking infused by the Babylonian system of this world portraying itself as a spiritual act of God but bearing no fruit or evidence of faith.

As you are in the Kingdom, that should be your outward experience in life. However, Babylon is antagonizing this process of spiritual naturalization as you try to gain a clear picture to of your inheritance in the Kingdom of God to produce tangible outward expressions of His life inside of you. Therefore, you have to take a stand against need-based mindsets and realize you are redeemed from lack, poverty, scarcity, and sorrow. Pray from a Kingdom paradigm in which provision inspires your words, not the slavish fear of need or inferior complex of lack.

You are not praying to gain anything; you already possess all things through the power of legal consent of God's Blessing on your life. Prayer is the strategic design of leveraging heaven's communication system to release and produce that Blessing in outward expression.

By clearly communicating God's will into every matter of your life, His Word is quick and sharp, maneuvering beyond the surface exterior to the root cause of every problem, severing every spiritual tie of disorder being manufactured by the kingdom of darkness into your life.

You are created to produce prosperity with your words. The life of God in you is ready to explode by streamlining God's thoughts into powerful faith-filled confessions that literally open the gates of heaven for real influence in your life. You have to be aware of God's divine plan of diplomacy in the earth in order for prayer to really work for you.

You have to learn to ask according to His plan as you discern His will for every matter and project His heart into your situation through words. Those words produce a sound and that sound is a language called "Life." When life speaks it edifies, it builds up and always encourages. It's a divine tool for producing the highest reality called truth.

When God asks us to speak the truth He is telling us to speak life so that we are always streamlining the communication sound and language system of heaven into our atmosphere. That atmosphere is interior, finding its roots within the soil of our thoughts as watering mechanisms able to produce a garden and spring of life through our sound. I want to ask you: What sound have you been making?

Indeed life and death are in the power of the tongue, but those are two language systems representing two governments at work in the earth. Every day each government is waging a bid for your tongue for policies to be released into the earth through the contract power of your words. That's right, your tongue is the pen of a ready writer, possessing spiritual ink that approves contracts of life or death to show up.

That is the system of prayer. It's a language system ruled by sound and operates through consistency, skillfulness, and accuracy.

I wrote this book as a resource and guide to help you better communicate God's sound into your life for heaven to operate in. This book is designed to change your total trajectory of praying and usher you into the Kingdom paradigm of praying that enlarges the view of what prayer really is, how it operates, and how to see continual successful results with it. There is a bid for your tongue that is taking place even right now, and the sound you make will empower the next contract that may be responsible for what shows up next in your life.

The more you realize that prayer is a principle of sound, you will learn how what you say all day long continues into a sound wave and frequency created when trying to connect with God. You are going to learn how words produce one consistent sound that determines what system we are under and what kingdom is prevalent in our lives.

As much as I'd love to tell you that every single prayer gets heard and that God is a loving God who answers all prayer, this is simply not truth. Scripturally, the Bible doesn't indicate this about God, rather it makes clear that there are several ways to pray wrong and when we fall victim to pitfalls of miscommunication we will not see manifestation of our desired requests.

Wisdom of how the Kingdom operates and how to operate its laws gives us the best position to produce winning outcomes, especially with prayer. However, you have to shift views and realize prayer is always happening. Realize that sound governs all creation and the universe is listening, not just when you make petition to God but when you are speaking all the time. That is why the Word teaches us to always speak life, sing songs of joy, and continue in thanksgiving and praise (Colossians 3:16) in all things, not just what we've prayed for.

If we really want prayer to produce real tangible results we must realize the joint partnership with God that takes place when we attempt to communicate with heaven. We have to learn to partner with God and leave the poverty mindset of self-effort and self-imposed praying behind. You aren't in need. And remember, need doesn't move God, faith does.

Praying from the defeated mindset is no longer an option for you. You must be accountable to the restored and redeemed nature of God's image flowing within your inner being. Grab ahold of it and begin to pray from the winning seat of prayer to gain your winning edge in life.

You are about to produce some prosperous outcomes with powerful declarations of life and forceful decrees of dominance. You have the authority to literally change outcomes by leverage God's winning system of the Blessing to empower your language and speech at all times. By training your tongue to the power of God's Word, wisdom, and instruction you are creating favorable outcomes that will become milestones of faith, building your confidence in God's ability to always do what He says no matter how big the request may seem.

This is your season of answered prayer, and the laws of the Kingdom are always working for you. Get ready to position yourself for clear line communication with the King and prosperous outcomes produced by the sound waves of heaven charging your atmosphere. You are created to win and empowered to succeed.

There is an overcomer inside of you waiting to be unleashed through a life of total victory and positive seeds of faith. You have been empowered with the entire communication system of heaven and its language of life called prayer. Now is your time to ask and now is your time to receive. Your empowered language of Kingdom communication is about to produce the culture of the Blessing system. God is restoring your thoughts with the right paradigm and perspective of a redeemed royal citizen of heaven. Right now you possess all legal rights to rule your world with the covenant blessing power of restored fellowship with God.

The Power of Pursuit: Kingdom Infused Praying

1

---

*But seek (aim at and strive after) first of all His kingdom
and His righteousness (His way of doing and being right),
and then all these things taken together will be given to
you.*

Matthew 6:33 (AMP)

Approach is Everything

There is an incredible story that emerges in the old
testament of the Bible about a young queen who rose to power, and
through her faith and brave petitioning she was able to spare the
lives of an entire race. Esther was faced with an important and life-
changing decision that would determine the lineage of her father's
house and existence of her people. Her cousin Mordecai had raised
the young Jewish queen, born Hadassah, since her early age. She
was well known for her beauty and attractiveness as well as her
heart of humility and service.

The time would come when King Ahasuerus, ruler of the
Persian kingdom that spanned 127 provinces from India to
Ethiopia, would began the search for his new queen. He issued a
decree that sent for all of the beautiful young virgins within his

kingdom to be summoned to his courts. Among those chosen was Hadassah. It wasn't long before she quickly became the king's favorite, rising to a position of influence much faster than of other women selected in the kingdom. Eventually, she would become known as Queen Esther, and great feasts were thrown with high honor in her name to celebrate the king's new wife.

However, this rags to riches story quickly becomes a tragedy from triumph experience, as things start taking a deadly turn when her cousin Mordecai, along with the entire Jewish race is sentenced to a mass slaughtering and execution as ordered by the king's highest ranking official, Haman. Now, it is up to young Esther to use her royal influence and power position in the kingdom to petition on behalf of her people that this decree be overturned and their lives be preserved.

It is important to note that in those times there was a significant difference between cultures then and now. It was illegal and punishable by death for the queen or anyone else to approach the king without being summoned by him. However, Esther knows that she is her people's only and final hope. And so with this pressure concerning the welfare of an entire generation upon her shoulders and a potential death penalty pending against her future, Esther must perform a courageous act of faith, and without summoning, approach the king on behalf of her people.

Can you imagine her thought processes as she enters the room? Step by step, she is bearing the weight her father's generation and sacrificing its hope of existence with each step closer to the throne room. Finally she opens the throne room doors and proceeds to approach the king. You can imagine the reaction of the people and the king's servants, aware that this woman has broken a constitutional law and gone directly against established order. Still, she continues to approach him with boldness and faith, that the king will spare her life before his guardsman raises his sword.

As she nears the king's throne, the soldier's sword is drawn but King Ahasuerus realizes that it is Esther who wants to address him. Conscious of his government's policy and aware of the risk Esther has taken to approach him, he quickly motions his sign of approval toward her by raising his golden scepter in her direction.

Esther reaches out and touches the head of the scepter and is welcomed by the king into his presence. Though Esther has gone against the government policy, his overwhelming favor with her superseded that law. So, the king simply asks, "What is your request? It shall be given to you, even half of my kingdom." Without hesitation, Esther invites the king and Haman, his official, to dinner. At dinner, Esther shares her heart with the king, making petition to spare her life and the lives of her people by reversing the policy made against them to be killed. Even though the command was being carried out by one of the king's most trusted servants, she boldly stated her demands, and the king responded by recanting the policy and executing his official.

Esther did not stop there. She petitioned, or requested, that a policy be passed that would protect her people from any attacks under the king's order. Subsequently, the king honored her petition and granted peace and protection to all of Israel. Mordecai was promoted to the king's palace, Israel was safe, and everyone rejoiced. One woman's courage and limitless faith was able to preserve and empower an entire race and generation simply through the power of petition.

Esther's breakthrough was not simply in the petition though, but in her bold and accurate approach to the king's throne. That boldness incited the king's grace and favor, positioning her to make unlimited requests directly to him. Regardless of the odds that may have been stacked against her, she continued in pursuit of the king.

Though her approach was not in alignment with earthly policy, it was most certainly aligned with the king's heart. Her bold approach, accurate pursuit, and clear petitioning resulted in immediate responses from her king ultimately releasing a new level of favor, opportunity, and breakthrough in her life as well as others.

The first and foremost element to a successful prayer life in the Kingdom of God is our view of the King, His Kingdom, and how we approach both. These may not seem like very important elements to prayer, but always remember that it is the small things that make big differences. Esther leveraged this principle to escape death and gain powerful advantage with her petition. And although we do not face the same level of tragic consequences similarly, our approach to God and His way of life can make the defining difference between getting answered petitions versus receiving unfavorable results.

So, what is the significance of how we approach God and His Kingdom? And how does that approach impact the effectiveness of our prayers? First let me explain what I mean by our "approach." The Kingdom of God is an invisible force that occupies and manifests through our spirit and subconscious being. Our spirit and heart are the center-point from which all Kingdom activity emerges in our lives.

Therefore, in order to effectively grasp and possess the Kingdom lifestyle, you must understand spiritual dynamics and the impact that our internal paradigms have on God's ability to move in our lives. In the simplest of explanations, our approach is simply the way we interact with God based on the attitudes and beliefs we have about Him.

Since the Kingdom at its core is an internal paradigm and perception that's ruled by heavenly jurisdiction we can then understand the impact that misaligned views and attitudes toward God's way of life are having on our spiritual successes, mainly in the area of prayer.

Referencing the story of Esther, it's important to point out again, that her bold approach (interaction based on belief) to the king was indeed against the law at the time, but in absolute alignment with his heart. In essence, he granted Esther access not based on the law of the land but based on the law that governed his heart and his will. In a kingdom there is no law higher than the law of the king's will.

It's also important to point out that one of the reasons King Ahasuerus allowed Esther to break that law forbidding her unsolicited approach to him was because it wasn't a law that Ahasuerus himself had passed. It was actually previous policy set in place by the kingdom before him. So although it was a previously instituted law, it didn't reflect the true will and desire of the king.

In the same sense, the correct approach to God and how to operate His laws of prayer will cause Him to supersede previous circumstances that have limited us for so long. Those limits are like previously established policies governing the systems of our world and our lives. Though these limited laws of life do not reflect God's will for us, they will remain in effect in our lives without proper alignment with His heart or an accurate view how His government functions.

It's important for us to grasp this, because although there are negative words spoken, financial restrictions, and other limitations of this earthly kingdom influencing our lives, we must tap into a correct pursuit and understanding of how God's Kingdom operates. That is how we access God's heart, wherein lies the King's law, which can supersede any force that would contradict God's plan for us. The law that governs God's heart is higher than any law or force that governs this world.

It is His will that is supreme, and by tapping into this supreme will we can boldly communicate a higher system of language into this earth realm that causes us to breakout and break through any bondage in our lives.

Examining Your Approach

I want you to take a moment to consciously examine some key questions:

- What is your overall view of God?
- How does this view influence your interaction with Him?
- Do you truly recognize that you're in a kingdom and you are in a relationship with a real king?
- Do you realize that God, who is King, has a specific function and order for prayer and how it is to be operated?
- In your most honest opinion, do you feel you have successfully aligned with that order to produce powerful consistent results with prayer?

Since you are reading this book you are most likely desiring greater results with your prayer life. And if you're anything like me, you are always looking for ways to achieve greater levels in the Kingdom so that you can produce a living manifestation of God's intended lifestyle for you. As a traveling speaker and life navigation coach, I often encounter hungry believers who are frustrated with the results they've been getting with prayer. Many feel like it just isn't working, or because God has not answered so many of their prayers, it simply just wasn't His will for them to have what they've believed for.

With so much frustration and so few solutions being offered, many of the unsuccessful prayer experiences of Christians have become seemingly hopeless battles they tend to give up on or simply end up reducing to the negative belief system that "if God wanted me to have it then I would have it." I become concerned when I hear God's children speak this way, because I know it's His will for us to have whatever we desire based on the promise of His Word.

As we examine the patriarchs of the Bible and their life stories, we witness the unlimited power of God's communication system. We see that when prayer is effectively communicated, anything is possible and nothing can stop you. In order to break through into a season and life full of powerful and effective praying, you have to be sure about this one thing: God hasn't changed His plan and there is a strategy for getting the results you need through heavenly communication in order to create the turnaround in your life you desire to have.

I want to encourage you that many times the answers to our greatest struggles are one revelation away. In this book we will uncover the mystery and revelation of communicating with heaven to alleviate unanswered prayer, remove all barriers and restrictions, and produce consistent results with the system of prayer in the earth realm.

With that said, I want to be clear that one of the greatest barriers that Christians are facing when it comes to unanswered prayer is the overall understanding of what prayer is, how it functions, and how to apply it. This misunderstanding is fueled by a misaligned perception of who God is, how His Kingdom functions and how we should pursue results with it. Notice that Jesus makes a significant statement about the Kingdom and how to get your needs met with it. In Matthew 6:33 (AMP) He says:

> *But seek (aim at and strive after) first of all His entire kingdom and His righteousness (His way of doing and being right), and then all these things taken together will be given to you.*

Getting back to the power of our pursuit and overall approach to the Kingdom, we clearly see here that we must prioritize our perception according the viewpoint of the King. Two things are made here 1) God is a King who rules in a Kingdom. 2)

God has a way of doing things in His Kingdom that we must align with to experience His best.

The word *seek* here is going to deal with more than just our aim, but what influences that aim and how we approach the objective of our aim. It implies the concept of accuracy, precision, and skill, which Jesus is plainly proposing are vital proponents to walking in the unlimited provision God has for us. Believe it or not, prayer requires skill and accuracy in order to be performed correctly. If God has made clear in His Word some do's and don'ts about prayer (which we will examine later in this book), it's important that we adhere to them; otherwise we will fall short in our prayer accuracy and language.

All of these components are essential to an effective prayer life and encompass our approach to God and His Kingdom. Whether or not our approach is consistent with the spiritual laws that govern the Kingdom as well as prayer, it is going to determine our aim and its accuracy.

However, Jesus said that when our aim is accurate and when our approach is aligned with God's will and intent, we will have anything we ask for and it will be given to us. Now, if you can recall King Ahasuerus' response to Esther's petition, which was: "*Ask what you want and it's yours,*" you'll notice the striking resemblance in both Jesus' statement and his. What's the significance? Precision, boldness, and accuracy are the platforms for those answered petitions.

What I am saying is if your praying doesn't seem to be effective or bearing the fruit you desire to see, maybe it's time to adjust your approach. It's time to gain an accurate bold perception of God our King and how to operate His Kingdom laws of communication. It all begins right here with your perspective and approach to His Kingdom.

A Kingdom Infused Approach

Without the right understanding it's easy to approach the Kingdom incorrectly. Many times when people seek God they pursue Him and His Kingdom objective rather than subjective. The main difference is having an outward perception versus an inward one. Remember that Jesus said, "The Kingdom is within you." That means we have the answers and we possess the power to manifest heaven's reality in this earth through the proper paradigm and internal lens of the Father.

Whether you realize it or not, God wants to awaken the Kingdom in you. Having the Kingdom in us not only provides great benefits of God's power and authority as His royal citizens but it also indicates that it operates solely off of the perception of the individuals using it.

Although God has an amazing plan for us, if we are misaligned with His Kingdom inside of us we will miss out on tremendous blessing.

So, if the Kingdom of God is within you, then the epicenter of all crises concerning God's plan for your life is happening within you. Though many Christians are not aware of this, our hearts are the command center for experiencing the Kingdom's quality of life. That means we must approach the Kingdom from a subjective standpoint rather than an objective standpoint allowing God's thoughts and internal paradigm to flow in you and through you. You have to allow God's principles to change and reshape you from the inside out.

In this book we will lay out some powerful principles to successful praying, but we will spend significant time adjusting your paradigm about how the Kingdom of God and how the Kingdom laws of prayer function as well. So, to clarify what Jesus is saying in Matthew 6:33, *if you approach the Kingdom any other way than it is designed to function and operate, you will not get successful tangible results; you will only reap a harvest of frustration and inconsistency.*

This means you must align with total agreement about God's supernatural life in you and how it operates to activate His presence. Therefore, you cannot approach the Kingdom with a self-imposed concept of how things should work or how God should move in your life. You will not see many results this way. Numerous people have tried to make the Kingdom of God what they want it to be. They have created their own approach to seeking God and tapping into His wisdom and grace.

This by definition is called religion and is the core cause of division and denomination in the church today. We could not quite figure out how to pursue and access the Kingdom God's way so out of frustration and desperation we created our own. Religion is basically seeking God with man's own ability rather than relying on the supernatural grace that's in every human being to guide him or her to correct alignment with our Creator, who is King. When a person uses their own methods of reaching God, they choose religion and self-effort rather than grace.

Consequently, a lot of teaching on prayer that exists today is founded on the basis of self-effort and not the picture of the rest we have obtained through God's sacrificial Kingdom. Without this understanding, individuals continue to engage in warfare, spiritual labor, and energy-draining exercises of what they believe is "praying in the spirit."

No matter how spiritual or effective it may seem, these kinds of attempts to connect with God only point to self-effort rather than directing us to the *rest* of Jesus where we are indeed a complete and finished work. If we can keep our "eyes fixed on Jesus" we can gain the right paradigm of our complete selves and obtain heaven's reality on earth. Remember that since God established man into His rest, everything we do in His Kingdom should be consistent with that. In other words, the culmination of every Kingdom pursuit should eventually point us back to our rest and finished work that Jesus has accomplished.

Subsequently, as Jesus proposes several times through His ministry, reaching heaven doesn't have to be hard as long as you are doing it the way God designed it. His proposal was that you must "seek first the Kingdom of God." The Kingdom must become one's priority in order for it to truly manifest and impact anyone's life. You cannot shift or create change in any area of your life where pursuit of God's Kingdom is not leading the change.

Even though this statement in Matthew 6 clearly gives clarity to the number one problem that mankind has with trying to rediscover God, it also reveals the root issues that practicing believers are experiencing every day in their overall pursuit of God's abundant life for themselves. When you pursue first the Kingdom, as I said, you must approach it the right way. For example, you cannot approach the Kingdom from the standpoint of just wanting miracles and signs. It doesn't operate that way and you will not access its gates; they will be closed to you. Neither can you approach the Kingdom expecting God to "fix it for you one time" if you are serious about seeing real results with His complete lifestyle.

The Kingdom of God is a system of life you must commit to living day in and day out. It was not designed to function on the basis of one-time happenings. It is a culture and philosophy of God's internal government that reflects His will, authority, and purpose. This supernatural government perpetuates itself into tangible activity in one's life through constant seeking and pursuing of its actual rule and government. When you pursue the Kingdom you aren't pursing religion or a one-time fix it cure. You are pursing a way of life that is a solution to everything in misalignment with God's will and intention showing up in your life. If you're serious about experiencing a real manifestation of the Kingdom of God then you have to commit to pursing it daily in your heart, soul, and mind.

So, you cannot decide what the Kingdom is to you. You must discover what it is, how it operates, and then consciously come into alignment and agreement with it. This is one of the ways you began to see its manifestations take place in your life. By agreeing with God about how His Kingdom and system of communication function we approach life in the Kingdom from the paradigm He intended for us to have from the beginning. That paradigm is a bold, skillful, and accurate approach to communicating with God and enforcing His will on our behalf in this earth realm.

So what is the Kingdom of God? If we are going to agree with and bring it to earth, then we better know and have a clear understanding of what it is. In my own words, the Kingdom of God is the divine influence of the will and intention of God manifesting in every sphere of our life. It's when we discover the source of God's nature lying within us by gaining His spiritual paradigm or lens of life.

We then must choose to allow that internal perception to become the governing force of everything we do. Once you begin to view matters and circumstances from of the paradigm lens of God, everything He sees (or intends) for your life must come into alignment with that same perception. Therefore, the Kingdom of God is an inward alignment and perception with God's supernatural way of life.

Right now, God is perpetuating His internal government through mankind by impressing people with accurate perceptions and appropriation of His principles and pre-established will. There is a Kingdom uprising taking place for those who will look up and "see" their deliverance drawing near. Essentially, you must see correctly into God's intention with keen accuracy in order for the Kingdom to have real impact in your life. Your breakthrough is tied to the correct Kingdom perspective about your situation. You must train and discipline your mind to continually live from that reality each day. Remember the Kingdom is within you, so you set the bar, and you get to choose the level of influence it will have in your life today. I can tell you that the more we're willing to yield to God's sovereign plan of inward governance, the more we'll experience the rights of our heavenly country. Through our position of Kingdom authority, heaven will begin to charge and release itself into active tangible expression for others to see.

Remember that God is not going to change, nor is He going to change His perspective or how His Kingdom operates. Your objective as a Kingdom citizen should be pursuing the King's heart, grasping His will and intent while allowing His internal paradigm to transform you from the inside out. Then you'll draw from the substance of a sure guarantee and promise in the King's Word to bless you in whatever you do, simply by searching, pursuing, and discovering the King's perspective in situations. When this happens, every circumstance and area of your life become legal jurisdictions for God's internal government to influence and have the final say in. Can you imagine? God having total rule and dominion to influence any area of your life at His will?

Can you imagine never having to worry about your provision or how you're going to meet your needs ever again? That's what happens when the internal government of heaven reigns in your life. You never again have to stress about how you are going to pay your bills or get the real breakthrough you desire to see. The Kingdom of God is your solution and releases heaven's provision package when you authenticate your citizenship by simply tapping into God's perspective, aligning with it, and allowing His way of doings things to govern your life.

Total alignment with this perfect perspective is called the Kingdom paradigm. It should influence how we approach God and how we see our lives in general. When we operate out of this mindset, heaven's doors are continually open to us and we can access what we need. The right perception is the power point for manifesting any and every one of God's purposes in us through His abundant reign and internal Kingship.

When we choose to operate outside of this paradigm, we view things from the world's perspective. That perspective, like God's Kingdom, is influenced by a paradigm, or way of thinking. The difference is that God is not the progenitor. That paradigm is like a box of limitation created by the walls of logic and fear-based thinking. When these limited perceptions are governing our perspective we easily slip back into a "fallen" state of thinking, which is the paradigm Adam came into after the fall. This is one of the most rarely understood truths about Kingdom manifestation, but if you will grasp this principle, it will impact your prayer life tremendously.

When Adam fell from grace he indeed lost his state of dominion of God's Kingdom in the earth. However, as we discussed, the center point for Kingdom operation emerges from an inward agreement and paradigm influenced by God's perceptions Himself. It's no different for the fallen kingdom, or Babylonian kingdom, that came into power when Adam relinquished God's rule and authority in the earth. Adam became subject to a new way of thinking, a new set of belief systems, ideas and perspectives powered by the mindset of its progenitor and king, Satan.

Simply put, Adam had changed kingdoms. Now, by taking on this new kingdom, he was functioning out of the fallen state or mindset of Satan who was cast from heaven and fell from grace too. Now if these two major spiritual kingdoms build their center points for manifestation within the heart as inward perceptions and paradigms that influence one's overall approach to every sphere of life, then Adam's change in kingdoms didn't occur physically, it occurred within a paradigm shift.

In terms of spiritual change and transformations, a paradigm shift happens within your spirit and impacts your thoughts with simultaneous processes of change. Both levels produce a way of thinking as a result of a spiritual metamorphosis taking place within one's heart and soul.

A paradigm shift is an exchange of one conceptual worldview for another conceptual worldview. And the difference in the worldviews will determine which government is ruling in your life. It only takes a limited perception or mindset empowered by fear for the Babylonian kingdom to come alive and reign in your life. You must decide what it will be.

This makes it vitally important that you understand that perception, or philosophy, represents one of the three main cultural blocks of influence that determine the existence and overall influence that a kingdom has on its culture. The other two are value systems and language.

In all actuality, prayer is a result of all three influences, but more specifically it applies to the realm of communication or language systems. If we are going to tap into a life of what I like to call "breakthrough prayer," we need to understand that prayer is our heavenly language, and how we operate that language system will determine the results we get when we are petitioning or requesting divine influence in our lives.

A Bolder You

So you see, our approach means everything when it comes to life in the Kingdom of God. We have to be sure that our inner perceptions are aligned with God's way of doing things and being truly inspired by the right system or kingdom. If not, it will interfere with the results we get when trying to connect with our command center in heaven.

Understanding this operation of Kingdom language will release a bolder and more confident you able to impact your overall approach to prayer. Knowing that you are doing it right and operating consistently with God's communication systems in the way He intended them to function can create a place of sure confidence in prayer. In this place, you become like Esther, unmoved by the distractions around you and unaffected by the odds you are facing.

You can feel boldness as you are aligning with the King's heart, the place where His perspectives and desires spring forth, and tapping into a higher supernatural law that can overcome and supersede any previous circumstance that riots against God's plan of favorable outcomes.

We have to understand that the wrong perspective of God and how His Kingdom operates will always influence our approach to Him and His way of doing things. Eventually, that misaligned approach is going to filter over into how we approach prayer and the results we expect to get from it. If there is one key to accurately approaching prayer we can gain from Esther, it is the understanding that the King requires boldness.

What is missing from most individuals' prayer life is a confident boldness inspired by the right perspective and assurance of viewing God and His language system correctly. Hebrews 4:16 encourages us that, like Esther, boldly approaching the throne is without a doubt one of the foremost Kingdom keys to answered prayer in the right season:

> *Let us approach therefore with boldness to the throne of grace, that we may receive mercy, and find grace for seasonable help.*

Hebrews 4:16 (DBT)

Now, we must be careful not to confuse boldness with some common practices and behaviors associated with prayer. This includes praying obnoxiously loud, extremely lengthy hours, along with wordy supplications. Believe it or not, individuals who pray like these are being persuaded with a belief system about prayer that didn't come from God. Boldness is a state of mind; it is a paradigm about what is rightfully yours and knowing how to skillfully go about obtaining it. It's having the heart of a "possessor," someone who doesn't approach prayer with any intention other than manifesting his or her specific desires or wants. Boldness cannot be taught; it can only be nurtured and cultivated by an atmosphere that is consistent with the Kingdom laws of prayer.

Referring back to the passage above, we must understand that a core secret to overcoming a major prayer barrier is also being revealed. That barrier is condemnation. Many people fail to understand the redemptive purpose and plan of Jesus' sacrifice and therefore lack the confidence and feeling of worthiness they should have. Satan uses the power of sin consciousness to exploit us and constantly attack our confidence with daily accusations of what we are doing wrong. You have to realize that when God sees you, He sees a finished work. Yes, I said finished. Jesus said it too, 2,000 years ago, and He meant it. Your job when the enemy points to you is to point to Jesus.

Don't get caught in the deception of needless warfare that has snared so many Christians. Satan is defeated; you are redeemed and the Blessing of the Lord is upon you. Now say so; agree with it and tap into God's complete and perfect perception of you. Regardless of how you may feel about it, you must use your faith to rise above your emotions. Allow God's redemptive plan to inspire a new boldness within you and what you expect to gain out of a consistent prayer life.

Have you gained consciousness of the boldness required by faith to truly tap into heavenly communication and enforce its divine influence in this earth? Do you think Esther gained her position to present powerful petitions to the king without functioning in a great dimension of uncommon boldness? You see, her life was dependent on that boldness, and that pressure released a level of courage that could supersede any written law of the land.

It's no different for you. Your life depends on the bold approach you are willing to take toward God and His system for answered prayer.

You need answered pending requests that can change your life and overall state of existence. If those requests aren't answered your life isn't going to change very much. So, allow this pressure, like Esther, to propel you into courageous levels, petitions, and acts of faith. Change your mindset, and stop thinking beneath your potential and position as God's favored. Picture yourself as a redeemed royal citizen of the most powerful country in the world, heaven. Whether you realize it or not, heaven is on standby and angelic reinforcements are waiting to show up and remind your situation who is boss. However, they are also waiting on you to recognize who you are in the Kingdom and to possess it.

They are waiting for you to gain the correct perception and internal paradigm of boldness concerning God's way of life and His approach to prayer. If you will agree with Him about how His Kingdom operates and skillfully apply His spiritual laws, you will unleash a supernatural you that's been lying dormant on the inside to be released.

Your uncommon boldness is about to release uncommon results. In other words, you are about to shift the unfavorable in your favor by recognizing the powerful principle of faith-filled fervent praying.

Power Concepts from this Chapter

❖ The first element to a successful prayer life in the Kingdom of God is our view of the King, His Kingdom, and how we approach both.

❖ Our attitudes and beliefs about God and His Kingdom impact our approach; therefore, it is important that we get rid of misaligned views and ways of thinking.

❖ When our aim is accurate and when our approach is aligned with God's will and intent, anything we ask for will be given to us.

❖ We have to allow God's principles to change and reshape us from the inside out.

❖ We cannot approach the Kingdom with a self-imposed concept of how things should work or how God should move in your life.

❖ You cannot decide what the Kingdom is to you. You must discover what it is, how it operates, and then consciously come into alignment and agreement with it.

❖ Boldness is a state of mind; it is a paradigm about what is rightfully yours and knowing how to skillfully go about obtaining it.

❖ Knowing that we are redeemed and free from sin consciousness will increase boldness and remove the barrier of condemnation.

Clear Line Communication:
Mastering Your Prayer Life

2

Prayer is not getting man's will done in heaven, but getting God's will done on earth.

-Richard C. Trent

Mastering Your Perception

By now you've probably realized that this approach to gaining more effective results with prayer is a little different than most. Again, prayer is the language system of heaven, which means your understanding of how the Kingdom operates determines what you pray, how you pray, and the results you obtain. While there are many credible books and other resources that have been written and designed to improve one's prayer life, I have found that a most devastating gap still exists between what we desire to have, what we pray for, and what actually shows up.

Even the most credible resources have aimed to teach individuals what to ask for, how to ask, and even how to war to get your results. Some of these things may work, but overall the gap is still prevalent in most Bible-believing, faith-filled Christians. Why? Well, as I stated earlier my approach to solving the issues of unanswered prayer is a little different. So I want to make a statement that may sound a little insensitive but bear with me: God hasn't answered many of our prayers because many of us aren't praying in correct alignment with God's Kingdom. That means how we pray, effective or ineffective, is a direct result of the paradigm position we have when we approach God.

I am thoroughly convinced that a solution exists for every person to get the prayers they need answered to produce the results they have desired to see for so long. However, could it be that the problem that exists isn't simply in our asking or declaration of the Word, but rather in our overall perceptive reality of what prayer truly is? Could it be our misunderstanding of God's purpose for prayer and how it is applied from a practical Kingdom point of view? I am convinced that many of us pray, and pray often, but very few have a real Kingdom paradigm function and understanding about how this spiritual operation is instituted in constituency with God's plan and purpose to prosper us in planet earth. Until individuals first become heirs of God's original intent and purpose for prayer they will never become actual beneficiaries of the inheritance of answered prayer. Yes, answered prayer is an inheritance for the royal heirs in the Kingdom of God. Answered prayer is not something that is supposed to be parlayed for by long practices and religious warring. Prayer simply is a paradigm needed to correctly communicate with heaven on earth's behalf in order to tangibly express God's will.

I certainly cannot speak for everyone, but in my own life I have gone through just about every frustration the average person encounters when trying to get results with prayer. There have been times when I felt myself asking God, when are you going to do this? Or, why didn't this prayer get answered? I understand that pain of disappointment when something you've really prayed hard for doesn't seem to come to pass.

The natural instinct is frustration, and continual encounters of the same inconsistency with effective praying which will leads to further frustration and disappointment in the believer's heart. Soon, we lose hope in God's ability to do the "big" miracles and reduce the power of prayer to small menial things we actually can do on our own.

Let me be straightforward in saying that prayer is not for things you can do on your own; it is designed to release the supernatural and perpetuate divine opportunities you cannot create yourself. This is how the Kingdom operates, through perpetual doors, initiated and activated by the accurate petitions of heavenly citizens in the earth realm.

So, the question that remains is: how do we fill in this gap of unanswered prayer? How do we put an end to the frustration of inconsistency and constant delay in our requests? We have to change our paradigm and perception of prayer to fully and completely align with God's attitude concerning prayer. It starts right here.

Have you ever heard the saying that "it's the small things that make a big difference?" Well, nothing could be said truer about praying. It has totally changed my life and blown my mind to understand how the seemingly small adjustments that we can make in our prayer life have the power to unlock the next dimension of grace and answered petitions. These small adjustments we will discuss will seem like nothing at first. However, that is the secret, not to overlook the small things. I want to challenge you as we look closer into the simple secrets and arrangements of the prayer paradigm to truly lock in on these bits and nuggets of information. You will be surprised at the unlocking power one accurate perception can have on a prayer request you been waiting to be answered for years. One of these small adjustments begins with our view of prayer versus God's view of prayer and how the two line up.

To effectively compare both viewpoints and perspectives we must determine which belief systems you have about prayer that may be affecting you negatively or positively. So, let's look at some examples of what prayer isn't so that we can truly identify what it actually is. For starters I'd like to ask you: What is your perception of a good prayer life? What is prayer to you? How do you believe it functions and operates? It is vitally important that you answer these questions honestly as it pertains to your constant awareness and perspective of praying. In order to truly dismantle unfruitful belief systems about praying you have to be clear about the things you believe now, so that it's crystal clear what needs to change.

After you've answered those questions I want you to take a look at the list below. I've comprised a list of what prayer is "not." Not every single one of these will apply to you, but as you read the list and you are truly honest with yourself, I am sure you will see some commonly held belief systems that you or someone close to you has probably had about prayer at some point in life.

Now, let's dispel more bad thinking about prayer so that we know what prayer is not.

Prayer is not:

- A religious act of worship
- Religious warring with Satan
- A system for communicating with God only when we need something
- A function designed to ask God about our needs
- A place to tell God about all our problems
- Wordy supplications that repeat the same things over and over
- A system deigned to ask God for money
- A system designed to seek miracles, signs, and wonders
- A system designed for one time fix it cures
- A system designed for you to out talk God
- A religious system of labor in which its effectiveness is measured by time or lengthiness

- Continual supplication about the same thing
- An instrument designed to be done publicly, loudly, or in the open for others to see
- Talking to God more than listening for instruction
- A reward system for most hours spent
- Simply a system designed for requesting things from God
- Designed as a one-man operating system
- A ritualistic act that ends when your petition does
- A spiritual power that comes on and shuts off based on your use
- A system that operates based on self-effort or ability

Now again, I believe that if you are truly honest with yourself, then you've probably recognized some views you picked up along the way that don't actually align with sound Kingdom representation of prayer's function. Like the rest of us, you have most likely adopted some belief systems about prayer that are not true. At this point, you may even be wondering, if prayer is not any of the above, then what is it? What real definitions of prayer still actually apply?

Let me first say this, if you are willing to receive this new paradigm concerning prayer it will change your life. Change can be difficult, a lot more than we realize. So, please understand that nothing I am saying is to seem insensitive or even the least bit arrogant. I am simply trying to help you dismantle bad beliefs you have concerning prayer so that you can release aspects of the Kingdom in your life that you have never experienced before. So again, now that we know what prayer isn't let's examine, based on the Word of God, what it truly is for once and for all.

Prayer is, by definition, the communication and language system of heaven. It is the sound of God's perception tuned by the frequency of hearing. Hearing what? His perfect will. You see, when we tap into that sound frequency of God's heart and learn to clearly communicate His actual will into the earth, heaven's communication system is in full activation and the laws of prayer have been effectively operated.

When Jesus departed from earth proceeding His resurrection He described several traits that new born again citizens of the Kingdom would have: He said they would heal the sick, raise the dead, and even drink poison and not die. But He also said they will speak with a new language or in new *tongues*. Now, I understand how many interpret this to mean diverse tongues. However, grammatically that is wrong, and this isn't what Jesus is referring to in this particular verse. By this tongue, He means the nature of a new language. Contextually it is the same use of the word He used when describing Satan in John 8:44 when He said:

> *He was a murderer from the beginning, not holding to the truth, for there is no truth in him. When he lies, he speaks his native tongue (language), for he is a liar and the father of lies.*

You see, in this passage when Jesus talks about native "tongues" He is actually referring to language, as in the official language of any country, government, or nation. In this verse he explaining that Satan, who rules the Babylonian kingdom, has a language system like any country, and it has been influencing God's citizens for too long. The point is that Kingdom praying is ruled by language systems and is by definition the clear and accurate use of heaven's communication.

Believe it or not, God is not the only one you can pray to. Once you apply the accurate belief system about prayer as a spiritual communication function, you have to realize that praying in the right "tongue" is key in order to make sure you connect with the right kingdom. In fact, when Jesus begin teaching His disciples on how to pray He explained to them to "pray to the father in heaven." Jesus was intentional and clear about giving this instruction because He knew that many of the prayers most people pray aren't real Kingdom prayers. In fact it's called the "Lord's prayer." Again, there are other types of prayer in the world and there are other cultures and religions that are open about using them.

However it is vital for us as Kingdom citizens, to check our "tongue" to ensure that we operate God's laws concerning this heavenly function correctly so that we connect to our source and not something else. You see, the truth is many Christians today speak with a cursed Babylonian language and don't' realize it. They don't understand how much they are engaging another kingdom. (We will look further into this later in this book.) As weird as this may sound, it is absolute biblical truth and a major concern Jesus was addressing in Matthew 6, when He warns us not to pray "as the pagans do" as it was their custom to pray long, unneeded laborious petitions in hopes that their sacrilegious efforts would move God. You are redeemed from that and you must not get locked into a style of praying Jesus didn't teach us. Unfortunately, today many believers tend not to take the communication system of prayer as seriously as they should. As a result, they continue to pray in a way that's misaligned with God's intended function of prayer.

As a result, more sorrow tends to show up in their life instead of blessing because they aren't speaking the correct language of heaven. Most are convinced that prayer is only active when they are attempting the physical part of what is generally called prayer. However, prayer is not determined by one's physical state. It's a spiritual posture, a paradigm position. Real prayer determines the entire base for communication with heaven. As Kingdom citizens, we have to learn that prayer is a law of language and is always active whether or not we are aware of it.

So, again what is the national language of heaven's country? It is called "Prayer!" Allow that to set in for a moment. Kingdom praying is more than just petitioning and making requests to God; it is the active function of the entire language system of heaven. Prayer is all round us. It's always happening in the Kingdom. It doesn't cut off just because you aren't conscious of it. It is spiritual law, and laws are always functioning with or without anyone's acknowledgement.

Think about it like this: many are not paying attention to the law of gravity throughout the day, but that doesn't stop it from functioning. It's the same way with prayer. It operates by divine or spiritual law in God's Kingdom. It's strategically set in place in order to enforce God's will in heaven and in the earth. Whether or not you are aware of it doesn't change its consistent function. The difference in your acknowledgement simply determines whether or not this is it's working for you. So again, you must ask yourself: am I operating the law of prayer accurately?

I hope that right now your paradigm about prayer begins shifting into greater dimensions, right here and right now. If you can adjust your internal paradigm of prayer from just a spiritual act being performed physically, to being an operational system of supernatural law and order, you will have opened the door to greater results with it. Mastering our perception of prayer begins with the life changing revelation that the Kingdom communication system is a heavenly language called prayer.

It's always happening! And I want to show you how the things we say all the time affect the results we get when we ask God for something. Our language is always active. Now the question becomes: whose language are we using and speaking most of the time? What tongue are we using? Because the language system that we depend on will determine what kingdom shows up the most in our lives.

Understanding the Official Language of Heaven

Here is something to consider: As a citizen of the United States of America, I am required to speak the language of my country, which is English. As a child growing up I was trained in school how to read, write, and speak in this language. In fact, language is one of the first things we learn as children growing up, how to talk as human beings, and secondly how to speak our country's language.

You see, from the starting point of a new believer's life, the moment they are born again, they come into the Kingdom and receive legal birth rights and citizenship in heaven. The first thing that we should be taught as new babes in Christ is our heavenly language and how to speak as Kingdom citizens. What has mostly happened in the church is the focus has not been on living in the Kingdom but trying to work "to get to heaven" after we die. Bad teaching like this has created false perceptions of salvation, causing God's Kingdom and His promises to go under valued being placed in the future and never within our grasp today. We are blessed *now* and God wants us to prosper *now*. Yet, Christians rarely understand that the very foundation Kingdom living is understanding God's original mandate to transform earth into a province of heaven.

With that said, our focus needs to be on teaching others how to live in this Kingdom of God while in the earth. This begins with one of the main blocks of cultural influence called "language." Now, I'm going to tell you that everything we possess as Kingdom citizens along with our legal right to tangibly possess and manifest those benefits begins and ends with our revelation of both speaking a new language and operating those spiritual laws of language called "prayer" in the earth. If I told you that your success as a Christian depended upon your communication ability through prayer, how would that change your perspective of it? It would probably intensify your focus and effort to gain clarity of what prayer actually is and how it really functions. Well, I am telling you that everything you possess as a redeemed citizen of heaven depends on your ability to truly rediscover God in you by connecting to an accurate prayer life.

It's important for you at this point to make the decision to view prayer in its correct context and dedicate yourself to mastering your native language as a citizen and earthly representative of heaven. This helps you to remember that you are in a Kingdom, it's your legal right to have your petitions heard and answered, and that as long as you manage the laws of prayer correctly, your other requests are sure to be effective and powerful too.

With that said, you must make the effort to remain consciously aware that your ability to operate and function in any government depends on the language you speak. The quality of life in any country is dependent on the language one speaks. A person must speak the native language of their country to effectively communicate, engage society, and operate successfully in that place. Likewise, when you master the language of heaven you ensure the best experience in this country.

It all starts with your understanding that now you have been translated out of one kingdom that rules in the earth, called the kingdom of darkness, and into a new kingdom, the Kingdom of light (Colossians 1:12). Your ability to articulate that language of light with God and to others will determine how often and to what measure the Kingdom of heaven shows up in your tangible reality.

Begin ruminating on this thought: *I am a citizen of heaven and I speak a heavenly language called prayer. Prayer is happening all the time, when I speak to others, to myself, and when I am speaking to God. Therefore, I'm committed to mastering heavenly language, according to the King's Word, so that His Kingdom is always showing up in my life.*

Transferred into the Kingdom of Sound

An interesting principle is in effect within the scripture I mentioned above in Colossians 1:12. The principle continues through verse 13:

> *For he has rescued us from the dominion of darkness and brought us into the kingdom of the Son.*

In the simplest of terms, God's Kingdom is a kingdom of light. The cursed world kingdom of this earth is called the kingdom of darkness. This means that the world is ruled and governed by one of two kingdoms: 1) heaven's Kingdom 2) Babylon's kingdom.

Every single person born into this world is born into the kingdom of darkness. That's why the scripture says, "We are born in sin and shaped in iniquity." This means we are all born into the dominion and rule of Satan's government here in the earth.

We are developed and cultivated by his nature, laws, and order. We learn to speak his language, think his limited thoughts, and as a result live beneath our potential as divine beings with the Blessing of God dormant on the inside of us. However, when we come into Christ, we receive baptism back into His Kingdom, and the eternal reign of heaven in our hearts becomes our governing authority. This happens through a conscious process of "translation" within our spirit being.

When the writer describes our citizenship experience as being "translated out of the kingdom of darkness into the Kingdom of the Son (light)," it means we literally shifted dimensions in the spiritual realm when we became born again. We changed kingdoms, not physically but spiritually. The problem that exists in the church is that many people don't understand they are in a different kingdom, heaven's Kingdom. Therefore, they still speak and act as though they are under the reign of the government they came out of called "darkness."

Now, these words "light" and "darkness" are very important. One represents the Kingdom of God and the other represents the kingdom of Satan. What they both have in common is that "sound" is the basis for how both kingdoms operate. You see, light, as referred to in Colossians 1:21, ripples back to Genesis 1 when God said, "Let there be light." That word *light* is not the sun, as commonly thought. God didn't put the sun in place until verse 8, along with all the other stars and constellations. When He said *light*, the Hebrew word there is *phonos*, meaning sound. We get the word *telephone* from it. What was God talking about when He said, "Let there be [sound]"? Well for one, it's not just any sound, He was transferring His sound to supersede all other frequencies.

God was translating His Kingdom into the earth by the power of sound waves and divine frequency. I want to pause for a moment to tell you that you cannot live in the Kingdom and experience real results without an understanding of sound and how God's Kingdom operates through it. Sound represents language; it is the spiritual wavelength that God operates on. So, when darkness is mentioned in contrast to the light, you are seeing an opposing kingdom reality that operates by a different sound called "darkness."

Here darkness represents deafness or dullness of sound. It means the opposite sound or language of the Kingdom of God. Why is this so important to grasp? Because now you can begin to understand how important it is to line up your words with the sound of heaven in order to really see God's Kingdom manifested through your prayers and petitions. When it says that we have been translated from one kingdom to the other, it's referring to transference of sound, which happens in our spirit. Now, you may be wondering: how this is possible?

It's literally a spiritual transportation that happens within us, which gives us the ability to tap into God's language and frequency so that we hear Him and imitate His exact sound in the earth. I want to really point this out because I believe one of the great barriers to tapping into the Kingdom is one's ability to actually perceive that it is within them. We have to realize we are spirit beings, made from words. The supernatural translation into God's Kingdom is immediate, and now it becomes our responsibility to enforce His sound through the right words as well as thoughts and conversations in our daily life.

When we do this, what God says about us is going to show up without limits because His sound will produce His "image" or light. So, notice that God had to translate His sound into the earth before He made man in His *image* before He did anything else. This is how the Kingdom operates and functions.

Whatever God does is only preceded by His sound being unleashed in that area. When this happens the Kingdom within us is literally "translated" into our atmosphere, and from there God's internal power and influence will begin to shift things in our favor. The Kingdom of God is translated through His sound, which is produced by His language in order to communicate the will of God accurately in the earth. So, to be clear, mankind is a sound, which is literally energy traveling through wavelengths. God literally created man by speaking him into existence through His divine sound. That means we literally possess within us the ability to operate in complete harmony and agreement with that sound.

Again, when the Bible says we have been translated from one kingdom to the other, it's through sound, in our spirit man. Because we are human beings made of spirit, our spirit is literally energy and sound waves. The translation or transportation into this new Kingdom takes place within milliseconds when a person crosses over from the cursed world into the Kingdom of Christ. It happens so fast that we cannot see it. However, it's real and the sound waves of heaven are operating within us waiting for us to cultivate them and produce them in the earth with clear articulation of God's Word through language.

Take for example Mary when the Angel Gabriel explained to her that she would give birth to the savior into the world, although she was a virgin. Mary's response was, "At your word, let it be as you have said." From there immediately she became endowed with Jesus Christ by her agreement with the Word. See, Jesus is the Word as stated in John 1. It also goes further to say that Word is light, and Jesus is the light of men. Again, here we are not talking about visual light, but the sound that releases energy, which in turn produces visual energy called light. So the Kingdom of the Son is indeed a reference to John 1, which means the Word, which is the light.

What did Mary do to tap into this massive blessing so quickly? She perceived God's sound and came into agreement with it, and it produced a physical harvest. And without hard laborious praying, she simply said "at thy Word" and her blessing was translated to her through her source, the Kingdom of light within her.

Your breakthrough blessing is one revelation away, and your ability to line up with God's sound will determine its release. I also want to go on record to declare this over you: Your days of laborious, drawn out, and energy-draining praying are over. You are about to tap into God's sound and release His authority over every area of your life.

Real effective prayer is determined by your ability to line up with God's sound and come into agreement with it, making the same sound so that the Kingdom within you can translate itself into this world and unleash a powerful inheritance for you. You have to remember that you are no longer in the kingdom of darkness, so be careful to examine your language at all times so that you aren't making its sound. Be careful you aren't complaining or constantly speaking negatively about things around you and in your life when they aren't going the way you want.

Prayer is not effective until what you are constantly saying truly lines up with what you are asking God for. You have been translated; though you may not always feel like it or be able to see it, you have changed kingdoms. You have the ability of God's nature reigning in your spirit. It's time to apply this understanding and enforce heaven's will on your behalf in your life. When circumstances do not line up with God's sound, don't agree with them or say what you see.

You'll be making the wrong sound and things will continue to conform to that what the situation is dictating. You have to speak a new sound over everything so that God can legally influence it at the right time in the right season. I just believe that all types of things are about to start turning in your favor. You are translated into authority, kingship, and unlimited power through the Kingdom of God.

The next time you are challenged to speak out of agreement with God's Word, begin declaring to yourself: *I am translated into the Kingdom of light. Therefore, I am only making God's sound and my circumstances are conforming to His image and His light within my spirit.*

The Partnership Paradigm

It's important to understand the ability that you possess to literally influence earth with the sovereign will of God and His Kingdom. The Kingdom really is within you. However, God is trying to reawaken your awareness to your royal citizenship so that your heart will begin to line up with His will (the place where His sound is released). As you perceive and agree with His will, you will be able to accurately articulate and enforce God's will concerning any matter for your life.

What I am saying is that one of the basic most powerful definitions of prayer is your ability to communicate God's will for any particular thing in your life. It's your ability to fine-tune your spirit to the sound of God's heart by tapping into His abundant will. When you properly discern God's heart for any situation, you then must align with it and declare that same perspective into your life and over your circumstance. When this happens, things around you will begin to shift and conform to God's favorable outcomes that He has predestined for you.

So again, a simple definition of effective prayer is one's ability to discern the will of God and properly communicate that will to produce in the earth realm. When we begin to say exactly what God is saying, everything in our lives will line up with what He is saying. So, what is God really saying about your life and situation. It's so vital that you ask yourselves these types of questions when shaping the power of a prayer paradigm. Jesus said it this way in John 5:19:

> *The words I say to you I do not speak on my own authority. Rather, it is the Father, living in me, who is doing his work.*

Now look at John 12:19:

> *Very truly I tell you, the Son can do nothing by himself; he can do only what he sees his Father doing, because whatever the Father does the Son also does.*

In both passages one thing is certainly made clear: Prayer is not a self-effort; it is a joint partnership with the God through the Holy Spirit. Many people have taken the wrong perspective of prayer in the sense that praying correctly is solely their responsibility. However, this is incorrect. In the Kingdom you have returned to the provision package of Eden where God meets all needs. This includes our spiritual provision as well. God is so abundant in the provision of His citizens that He always has a plan to meet every need, even the need of answered prayer.

So, you have to shift paradigms from self-effort to a joint effort with God to receive and relay His will properly in the earth realm over any circumstance. You and God are on the same team and He is simply streamlining His voice through the frequency of His sound directly into your heart concerning His will for all matters in your life.

When you grasp this concept you will no longer feel the need to bear the weight and burden of getting your prayers answered; you will learn to perceive accurately what God is saying about a situation and based on that perception you will clearly communicate His will into the earth. This is the power of manifesting God's will in your life, which is one form of Kingdom manifestation.

Remember, prayer is joint power. It is a partnership with Jesus Christ to tap into His sovereign will by operating the supreme laws of communication. He is trying to enforce His will through us. This is so *as it is in heaven* things will also be in the earth. This understanding should help you shift into the accurate prayer paradigm needed to really make a difference with heaven's communication system.

Now, referring back to both scripture verses above, Jesus is clearly establishing how effective communication in the Kingdom happens. He says the basis of His effective results is that He is able to "hear" and "see" what the Father is doing. This immutable truth challenges us to examine more clearly: What is God saying about my life. What is He up to?

Both verses here deal with perception, as in sound, referring back to Colossians 1:13 concerning the Kingdom of light. God's heart must be perceived, and in order to do that we need to clear up bad perceptions we already have about Him, His Kingdom, and how the Kingdom laws of prayer are to be functioned and operated.

So we are partnering with God in the earth to establish and enforce His will for us. This is great news, because Jeremiah 29:11

reminds us that God's plan is to prosper us. That means God's wants us to excel beyond all odds. So, why has God tied the effectiveness of prayer to the ability to perceive His will? Because His will is the best thing for us. He knows His plan and if we trust His plan over ours, we will get the breakthrough we have been seeking and more.

This doesn't mean that God doesn't care about what we want. In fact, He desires us to have all that we want as He tunes our hearts. However, He does not want us to limit what He can do. Let's be clear about this, God wants to bless you! When He says His plan is to prosper us that literally means the most favorable outcome. No matter what it is, God always wants us to come out on top. He always wants us to triumph with positive outcomes. So if you are going to tap into God's system of prayer you need to know deep in your heart that God's plan is bigger and better than yours and it is a plan to bring you into the best possible outcome. God is not concerned with what's good only; He wants what is best for you. You have to believe this and trust this because when you do His will, it becomes activated and accessible on a greater dimension as we depend upon His prosperous plan.

This is the power of partnering with God. He partners with us to communicate His plan in the earth, but we also join with Him to produce the results we desire as well. In other words: we have got to learn to work with God. Notice what it says in Romans 8:16-17 (AMP):

> *The Spirit himself testifies with our spirit that we are God's children. Now if we are children, then we are heirs—heirs of God and co-heirs with Christ…*

Jesus wants you and I to know that we are literally partnering with Him to advance His Kingdom purpose in the earth. I am telling you that if people can grasp this partnership paradigm of prayer, they will learn to tap into God's will for prosperity and prosperous outcomes for every area of life. To put it plainly: God is looking for someone to partner with.

I will never forget the time in my life that I was very frustrated with unanswered prayer. I began to seek God for understanding as to why it seemed like He only answers prayers when He feels like it and not all of them. You may be able to relate to this feeling, and truthfully it can get pretty disheartening to be the children of God but always seem to be hitting and missing with answered prayer.

Finally, in the midst of my frustration and during a preaching engagement God gently spoke to me and said, "You are selfish." I was thinking, "What! How can you say that?" After I was finished speaking I rushed home and begin to seek God's Word, waiting for Him to explain to me what He meant. Though the statement bothered me I could tell He was about to unleash and download a life changing principle to me. He said, "You are only concerned about what you want. That is why many of your prayers don't get answered. I want to partner with you so that we both are able to accomplish our desires."

Then He asked me, "Will you partner with me?" At this point I was impacted because now I had seen God's heart concerning prayer and I began to clearly understand the cause of frustration for many believers concerning prayer today.

We have to learn that partnering with God is the most powerful thing in the earth. We are joint-heirs with Christ and we must learn to conform our will to His so that God's plan is enforced through us, and in doing so we will always end up on top. This is what the scripture means in Romans 8:28:

And we know that in all things God works for the good of those who love him, who have been called according to

his purpose. For those God foreknew he also predestined
to be conformed to the image of his Son.

Notice God strategically "works" things together for *our* good, not *His* own. This is important. See, you have to understand that He works things together for us and in our favor, according to His purpose or plan. Nevertheless, God works with us; He partners with us to bring our desires to pass by conforming us to the "image" of His son. What does this mean? Again, the word image is going to reference the Garden of Eden, which we find in Genesis 1, when God made man in His "image" or His light. Here we are talking about the image produced by sound.

So when God says He is conforming us into the image (sound) of His Son, who is the Word, which is light, this is congruent with Colossians 1:12-13, that we have been translated from the kingdom of darkness to another Kingdom with a different sound, called light. Here that translation within our spirit takes place. We immediately exchange wills with God and the Kingdom comes alive for us to manifest and enforce through clear communication of God's promises and plan in the earth. What I am saying is that the only way to prosper in our lives in the Kingdom is to conform to God's plan to prosper us.

However, we must connect to the Kingdom that is within us through God's sound and His language system. By aligning our hearts with heavenly communication, we receive revelation of what to pray and how to go about reaping the harvest for it. Here, our lives are being gradually reshaped according to the original provision plan of Eden, where there is no labor or sweat involved, only the peaceful process of partnering with God to manifest His unlimited and sovereign purpose for us in the earth.

Power Concepts from this Chapter

❖ Prayer is not for things you can do on your own; it is designed to release the supernatural and perpetuate divine opportunities you cannot create yourself.

❖ Prayer is the communication and language system of heaven. It is the sound of God's perception turned by the frequency of His will.

❖ What we say all the time effects what we get when we ask for something or declare, because our language is always active.

❖ The language system that we depend on will determine what kingdom shows up the most in our lives.

❖ God literally created man by speaking him into existence through His sound; therefore, we possess the ability to operate in complete harmony and agreement with God's sound.

❖ Real effective prayer is determined by your ability to line up with God's sound and agree with it, making the same sound so that the Kingdom within you can influence your earthly affairs.

❖ Prayer is not a self-effort; it is a joint partnership with the God through the Holy Spirit.

The Paradigm of Prayer: Mastering Communication

3

The Posture of Prayer

There is no doubt that God's plan will prosper us every time we access our Kingdom authority through His will to enforce blessing and promise in our earthly affairs. You can be sure that any problems presenting themselves in the face of Kingdom citizens doesn't stand a chance against the power of accurate skilled praying. The more confident you become in God's sovereign will to prosper you, the more strategic and consistent you'll become at gaining His perception and drawing from His heart to find the solutions to life's problems.

There is no circumstance that you are faced with that your King hasn't already created a solution for. The strategies are there, wrapped in divine revelation waiting for us to access them through agreement with God's sound. This makes trusting His plan to prosper us an essential key to developing a healthy and successful prayer life.

Our mindset about prayer has to become aligned with the power of sufficient grace. God's Kingdom within us supplies every resource needed to unleash heaven's actual authority into complete manifestation. That manifestation is our key to thriving. We need to be constantly aware of the grace of abundance within us through our divine nature. This means we are whole, full of peace, and at no time are we ever in lack, shortage, or scarcity in any area of our life, regardless of how it seems

Now, I realize that it's possible that your situation may be dictating otherwise. However, you have to make the decision to be persuaded by the reality of God's Kingdom and abundant grace within you that provides a pathway to solutions and positive outcomes every time. This is what I call gaining your posture of prayer.

In the beginning of this book, I mentioned that the boldness and approach of Esther were both key elemental forces to her breakthrough when she petitioned to the king. Part of what should influence our bold approach is our understanding that God has restored us back to our original position in the Kingdom as divine beings with all provision met spiritually and materially. There are absolutely no limits that exist on the lives of Kingdom citizens, except for the ones we perceive are there.

How we view God and our approach concerning prayer is distinctly tied to our overall self-evaluation. We must have complete certainty that Eden is restored in us so that we no longer pray from a defeated stance. We are not fighting to gain the upper hand or winning position. We are simply adjusting and tuning our hearts to the sound of God, tapping into government policy already set in place that is designed to produce our winning in life. This is the posture for effective praying. You have been translated back to the right hand of God. You no longer should pray out of need, you should now pray from the perception that needs are met and that you are allowing the force of God's spirit to guide and navigate you into the proper place for your breakthrough.

I am telling you that it is an entirely different perspective than praying with the attitude that we are in need and God has to do something for us. This makes an enormous difference in how effective we are when it comes to praying for solutions. Agree that within your heart the curse is broken and you no longer have to see yourself outside of God's original plan, which is wholeness from meeting all of your needs. Now our provision comes through divine revelation of where His solution rests, where the harvest is, and His strategy for reaping that harvest now.

Prayer Protocol

With that said it is time to begin examining the prophetic protocol of praying. First and foremost, our intention has to line up with God's intention or we will be praying in vain. This starts with our attitude and boldness of approach, which leads me to an important principle of posturing for prayer. Again, our boldness should flow from our understanding of who we really are in the Kingdom, that we are co-heirs with Christ reigning in His government now. We are legal representatives of heaven in the earth realm, given full authority by the King to dominate this world through the enforcing of His will.

Furthermore, that boldness is inspired by the Kingdom revelation of having every need already met. When we have a Kingdom paradigm about who we are, it changes our approach and overall certainty with prayer. It enforces heaven's belief systems about us and our circumstances. It teaches us to pray from the posture of a winning position rather than the defeated perspective of a losing seat.

Now, I am sure many of us do not approach prayer thinking, "I am defeated and lowly." That's not what I am trying to address. However, when we pray outside of a Kingdom paradigm we allow traces of the fallen Babylonian kingdom to influence how we see ourselves and our overall position in terms of effective praying. When this happens we take the defensive end of praying versus a winning edge. And when it comes to success with prayer this makes a big difference.

Instead of releasing Blessing we find ourselves fighting the enemy for breakthrough. Many times individuals feel prayer has to be an aggressive activity that requires loads of energy and great lengths of time to actually see real results. This is what happens when we are praying outside of the Kingdom paradigm; we don't realize we have already won every battle and we already possess every solution and winning strategy. The Bible is clear that we are wearing the victor's crown and sitting in the seat of champions. But when we don't assume our correct position we will find ourselves fighting battles that we've already won.

The prophetic protocol of prayer is designed so that we pray from a bold approach based on the King's original winning intent for our lives. This protocol says if we want to access God's heart and His will for our lives then we first need to agree with who He says we are and what He says we have.

We absolutely should be coming to the throne with the mindset that provision is met, God has already provided a solution, and we only need understanding of the strategy for reaping our harvest. Now, please remember that prayer is not simply the act of approaching God and making requests; it is a law that functions in different forms. Approaching God is in reference to making petitions, a function of prayer we will examine later in this book. Prayer is always happening. It is law; it is the language of heaven, which demands that this protocol is always active in us.

So, the prophetic protocol is designed to position you to function in clear communication with heaven through the right paradigm and perspective of your power position expressed through your confident and bold approach. When we catch this and fully grasp this principle we are now in the correct posture of praying and we can approach God with the right attitude, self-image, and bold expectation that will lead to dynamic results in our prayer lives.

In a short review, the prophetic protocol establishes ten concepts and principles about prayer and how you should position your mind to approach God:

1) Gain a Kingdom paradigm of prayer.

2) Understand your position as being fully restored to the unlimited rights of Adam before the fall.

3) Realize you are a Kingdom citizen with full authority to access God's will and release it in this earth.

4) Understand that as a divine being you have all needs met, so there is never a need to pray from a position of worry or fear of any lack.

5) Realize that you fully possess every strategy for a winning solution.

6) Know that your prayer will simply release a strategy for reaping the harvest.

7) Avoid praying from a defeated standpoint by leveraging your winning mindset.

8) Understand that you wear the victor's crown and that you are seated in the champion's seat, and determine to pray from that position.

9) Agree with God about who He says you are and what He says you have.

10) Commit to always remain conscious of this protocol when approaching prayer.

The Language of Listening

Now that you have begun gaining the correct paradigm about communicating with God and your position of legal authority to access His plan, you can approach God with an aligned heart that is bold and ready to receive His commands along with revelation of His strategy to enforce His ultimate plan in your life. What happens from here is a simple and basic concept, yet probably the most important divine force of prayer: the concept of listening. This is probably the most overlooked and unexercised principle of the law of prayer, but learning to perceive God is listening, and it really isn't as difficult as many people think.

Remember you are now posturing yourself to receive from God. You have gained the right paradigm about who you are and your ability to receive downloads from God's heart to yours. You have been translated into the Kingdom of light, and God's sound is in you ready to be translated into earth to influence any and all of your affairs. As you incline your inner ear to the wavelength of heaven within you, God's picture is going to become clear for you to draw from to create tangible expressions in your life.

Now, you have to believe with all of your heart that by being translated back into the Kingdom of God and positioned in the authority seat with Christ, you possess the supernatural ability to hear and connect to God. Jesus makes a remarkable statement concerning the law of listening in John 10:27 (AMP):

> *The sheep that are my own hear and are listening to My voice; and I know them, and they follow.*

The principle of hearing is the essential key to answered prayer. For too long, individuals have operated under the notion that it is our job to create the right prayers that need to be prayed. When this happens we operate outside of a Kingdom paradigm, relinquishing our partnership rights as joint-heirs with Jesus Christ.

When we make prayer a self-effort rather than a combined effort with the Holy Spirit, we are relying on our own ability to pray right or come up with the right words, rather than listening and receiving a divine download by grace of what needs to be said. Through the Holy Spirit, who is your internal guide and compass, God wants to help you perceive His sound so that you can receive downloads of revelation concerning His heart for every matter.

Once you've tapped into God's perceptions, you can agree with and reflect those same thoughts into the earth as you echo

God's responses clearly. By doing so you're creating a channel of influence for heaven to operate through God-inspired words and petitions. This is always how prayer was designed to operate.

Remember that prayer encompasses the entire command center for heavenly communication. Whether you realize it or not, you are praying right now as you read this book. How? Because you are subjecting yourself to heavenly communication. Prayer is not just what you say, it is also listening to God and receiving downloads that will lead us into divine destinies.

I like to put it this way: outside of the Kingdom paradigm, prayer is generally thought of as us talking to God. However, when we access the Kingdom paradigm of prayer, it becomes God talking to us. Many people approach prayer with the idea that they need to speak first, but the Bible is clear in so many scriptures that we are to be slow to speak and to listen first. One of the reasons for this is because without a real spiritual navigation in prayer, we pray wrong.

Even though we may feel we've prayed the most energetic and effective prayer, most of the time we have only produced exhaustion through self-effort. This is not the original design of the law of prayer. It is natural to think this way, as it is what most of us have been taught that we need to speak the most when praying; however, answered prayer is not a weight we as believers bear, but a result of divine communication that naturally links heaven to the earth realm in order to accomplish an already existent plan set in place.

These two perspectives can make a very big difference in the success you experience with making petitions to God. First we need to be clear on what it means to listen to God, what His sound is, and how to perceive that sound. From here we can lay out some practical principles as to how these function in the overall intent and design of prayer. Again, light is sound, as we've previously discussed. That sound is really a perception that we take on through the Kingdom of God in us. This sound tunes our spirit as directed and guided by the Spirit of God. Through Him, God lives in us. His frequency is available to us, and through the practicing of principles concerning Kingdom praying, we can illuminate our hearts with the right wavelength to discover God's supernatural sound He wants to commutate to us.

Without that perception our connection with Him is ineffective and our ability to receive revelation and understanding are paralyzed through a dullness of hearing. This is the kingdom of darkness trying to darken our ability to receive translations from heaven to oppose God's sound in the earth. Nevertheless, you are translated into God's Kingdom, and the high position you have in God's government gives you the authority to rise despite the spiritual gravity of the world's government. You are also empowered to clearly communicate heaven's will in the earth through sound revelation accessed through the law of listening.

To go a little further, I want to point out some important principles concerning the laws of perception in the Kingdom. Matthew 13:11-16 (AMP):

> *And He replied to them, "To you it has been given to know the secrets and mysteries of the kingdom of heaven, but to them it has not been given."*
>
> *For whoever has [spiritual knowledge], to him will more be given and he will be furnished richly so that he will have abundance; but from him who has not, even what he has will be taken away.*
>
> *This is the reason that I speak to them in parables: because having the power of seeing, they do not see; and having the power of hearing, they do not hear, nor do they grasp and understand. In them indeed is the process of fulfillment of the prophecy of Isaiah, which says:*
>
> *You shall indeed hear and hear but never grasp and understand; and you shall indeed look and look but never see and perceive. For this nation's heart has grown*

gross (fat and dull), and their ears heavy and difficult of hearing, and their eyes they have tightly closed, lest they see and perceive with their eyes, and hear and comprehend the sense with their ears, and grasp and understand with their heart, and turn and I should heal them.

But blessed (happy, fortunate, and to be envied) are your eyes because they do see, and your ears because they do hear.

In these verses, Jesus paints the perfect picture that explains the pitfalls to receiving from God and perceiving His voice. In essence, He is saying that although Christians possess the ability to hear and see God, many do not, because of their inability to rise above their dullness of perception. This can only be broken with new truth.

That dullness of hearing has been coached into the minds of many Kingdom citizens who have become mistaken about the position we hold when praying, what posture to take, and how to approach God to gain real results when communicating with Him. You see, the Spirit of revelation knowledge, Jesus proposes, has been freely given to all of us. However, those who refuse to see a perfect picture of God's grace and rest within us will continue to operate in a mindset ruled by the spiritual laws of the Babylonian kingdom. They will continue to pray wordy prayers and think on the defeated end of praying. Here, the dullness of hearing really begins to take effect as the heart of the believer becomes arrested with bad concepts of praying and overwhelmed with continuous repetition of ineffective prayers. This makes it difficult to receive revelation this way. When we feel prayer is designed for us to always make a deposit rather than receive one from the Holy Spirit, we are not positioned to correctly tap into revelation that can change our situations.

I remember the time I was in need of a new car. The lease on my current vehicle had just expired and I had watched God work an amazing miracle to ensure that I paid that lease completely and on time. My faith had been impacted by revelation concerning the Kingdom and the material blessing I had access to through my agreement of faith with the Abrahamic Blessing. Within a couple of weeks of turning in my vehicle, I begin to make the confession about receiving a new car, this time one I would own and not lease.

In the middle of my confession, God stopped me. At this point I was getting used to God's divine interruptions; whenever I was praying wrong He would stop me and counsel me how to ask. He reminded me to listen first and see what was on His heart concerning my situation.

I received a revelation about a car God wanted to give me, but I wasn't sure what kind. I knew I always wanted a Cadillac but at this point I simply received by faith that according to God's plan I would receive a new car. The next day while I was running, I saw the emblem of a Cadillac flash in my mind. I saw it so clear that I paused from running to focus in on the voice of God. Sure enough, I heard "Believe me for a Cadillac." I responded, "Lord I agree and receive."

I was okay at this point, until He said, "I meant believe me for one today." This was hard to receive. Sure I could believe God for a new car, but in the same day?

I began to picture God's rest within me and reminded my heart that in the Kingdom there is no labor and that I was not going to place any limits on God. I remember focusing my thoughts, taking a deep breath and simply declaring, "Yes, I receive my new Cadillac today!" I thought that was it, but again in my heart I felt like God was telling me that it would come that evening around 7:00. At this point I was only depending on the sound of heaven in my heart and God's ability to bring me into my harvest based on His plan of provision.

So, later that evening at 6:55 pm I received a phone call from an individual who owned multiple vehicles. He told me that he wanted to give me one. I kindly asked what kind of vehicle it was and he said, "A Cadillac." I went that same week to pick up my new car, free and clear with the title in my name. The most amazing part is that several months after sowing this vehicle to me, the individual received a major financial harvest of $20,000 for some property damage that he wasn't even aware that he had. He and his wife had literally received money for damages on their property that was done before they moved in.

I want to place emphasis first that this is God's will and intent for his citizens. Jesus died in order to break the contract that was keeping us out of constant fellowship with God's heart. We are redeemed from the spirit of labor and God desires to leverage prayer as an access point of communication to instruct us clearly on how to receive blessing. The breakthrough was tied to my ability to listen to the sound of God's heart and receive revelation as to where my harvest was. You see, just like in my situation, God is always saying something about our circumstances, and it becomes our responsibility to learn what that is through patient listening and receiving revelation knowledge.

You have to remember that His translation of sound is happening in your spirit, and by allowing God's Spirit to navigate your senses you will eventually *see* what God is doing and *hear* what God is saying about your life. Second, I want you to see how someone's giving to meet my need was distinctly tied to God's plan to increase and bless them with more. This is why trusting God's plan is so important. When we partner with God and listen for His plan it is always bigger than us and connected to His divine system to impact someone else's life.

So, hearing or seeing is your ability to perceive what God is doing or what He is saying about the things on your heart. It's your ability to connect to God's will by divinely inspired communication with Him. You don't have to work for this; you naturally possess this ability through the Kingdom of God in you, within your new born-again spirit.

You have to commit yourself to make prayer more of a listening effort than a talking one. It was never designed for us to out-talk God, yet many Christians function like this. Wordy prayers are not necessary when we line up with God's perception and receive downloads of revelation that will lead us into God's plan for obtaining our promise. As we will examine more closely in chapter 8 of this book, Jesus warns believers about the pitfalls of praying with wordiness and repetitiveness.

We need to understand that in the context of spiritual matters this is a dangerous thing for us to do as it involves self-effort and striving, along with the constant release of a sound wave that didn't flow from God's presence. Instead, allow the Holy Spirit to tune your perception by simply praying this: *Father, I thank you that I am tuned to your sound, and your perceptions have become mine. Now I activate the law of listening so that I may hear and see your heart concerning my life.*

If you prayed that you should expect a new frequency to emerge within your spirit. Just begin to believe that as your paradigm of prayer is shifting to an attitude of listening, God is about to download strategic revelation to you that will change your life and the results you get when communicating with Him. Prepare for a new sound to invade your heart.

Now, it is important that I point out many people trigger these laws of prayer without knowing it. According to the science and operation of force, awareness is not a requirement to operate any kind of law.

Think of gravity for example. Most people aren't aware of the force they put on it throughout the day but it still functions for them the same. It is like this with the spiritual law system of the Kingdom, and hearing God sometimes is something we tap into without really knowing how to do it again.

I want to encourage you that listening, hearing, and perceiving God's sound are all divine laws that operate in the communication system of prayer, and your ability to learn them and become consistent with them will unleash a life of answered prayers and fulfilled promises.

Breaking Down Listening Barriers

Turnaround is never as far away as it seems; however, we have to remember the God-nature that is in our spirit and that we have the ability to enforce that nature with legal authority. If we are going to learn how to continually draw from the wellspring of divine life within us, there has to be a commitment to take a faith stand against every negative fear-based way of thinking and speaking.

What we hold onto that doesn't agree with God's view or perception will eventually become invisible snares that inhibit us from being able to fully practice God's presence and receive downloads of truth from Him. Those snares become what I call "barriers to listening" and many believers today suffer from these barriers because they have failed to fully agree with God's sound and how to tune their heart to His frequency. These barriers can show up in many different ways. They are strongholds in the mind that keep people from being able to line up with the inner picture God has created of them within their spirit. If there is anything your enemy wants to block, it's your true divine and royal perception of yourself.

By definition, a barrier is something blocking access. Mindsets of negativity and opposition are constantly trying to gain ground in our lives so that we will continually to be ruled by another language and kept out of our inheritance. However, we have a winning solution within God's plan to position us to emerge as unshakable and unlimited beings in the earth realm. It is so powerful that not even hell and all of its demonic magistrates would be able to keep you out of the blessings of God.

This is what Jesus meant when He said, "On this rock I will build my church and the gates of Hell will not prevail against it." You see, Babylon is full of barriers and spiritual strongholds. God wants you to know today that through the knowledge of the Kingdom you never again have to give Satan any ground in your life.

However, the source of Jesus' church or government operation in the earth was a "rock", which is revelation. That revelation only comes as a result of God's perception by way of listening. When we understand that revelation causes us to become an unstoppable force in the Kingdom, we will break through every barrier of listening into the limitless potential we possess as Kingdom citizens.

What beliefs do you have about hearing God that you feel may be limiting your ability hear Him? Realize you have the sound system of heaven, and the anointing within you to destroy every hindrance from accessing it is about to be unleashed. Today, start believing and agreeing that God has something to say to you and you are ready to hear it.

It's time to begin declaring: *I am a barrier breaker and there are no limits on my ability to listen and hear from God.*

The Hidden Power of High Impact Prayer

Your ability to receive downloads of information from heaven takes place within your spirit through the Kingdom that lives in you. This ability determines your overall effectiveness with prayer, as heavenly communication depends heavily upon your capability to understand what God is saying and to streamline those exact things into the earth through words.

That's high impact praying. When you can really gain a clear picture of the authority that's inside you, you can focus and concentrate on it along with your ability to tap into God's intrinsic presence. From here, you can begin to channel that focus into a consistency of thoughts and ideas that all cultivate the mentality that "God lives in me." This adds force to your prayer power, as the potency of your words is drawing directly from a streamline connection with the Spirit of the Kingdom.

Think about that. Your words have the ability to be streamlined with the consistency of God's heart. What you say and the things you petition have real authority to overpower the systems of this world and any limitation coming against your life. This understanding creates fervency and an attitude that all of heaven is listening when you speak. High impact praying begins with high impact faith. As you engage this mentality, be aware that you are creating an atmospheric shift around you.

Your energy will intensify when you connect with God because your mindset will have shifted from the power of your will to the power of a joint effort with the sovereign will of God.

There are many examples of high impact praying in the Bible. This is where individuals have gained their personal power of prayer through the force of petition. These petitions, however, all have something in common: they are short and brief. High impact praying is like a spiritual jolt you release into the earth through the empowering belief system that God is in you and you aren't praying alone.

Allow this understanding to charge your thoughts and words the next time you approach the throne of grace with petition. Realize that God wants to pray through you and with you so that He can release His supreme sound waves in the earth to give you greater dominion over your life.

Take for example things we say to people when we are extremely upset. Did you know a recent study on emotions and words proves that what we say when we are emotional have more impact on others and ourselves than what we say when we are not?

Well, what happens is when we are emotional we are determined to release our words with as much energy and meaning as possible. When we do this we are actually operating in a spiritual law unconsciously. And again, because spiritual laws only function by force applied, knowledge of using them is not a requirement for them to be active.

We have to apply the same principle with the Kingdom of God when we pray for high impact results. Instead of using negative emotions, we should empower ourselves through the spiritual energy harnessed by complete confidence in the Word of God and that the words we release have the ability to go out from us and have a cataclysmic effect on our circumstances.

We can leverage a thought life infused by the reality that heaven's substance is within us through God's Kingdom and we have the ability to translate its unlimited influence into the earth we live in. As you allow your thoughts to be charged with this principle, focus your thoughts and tune your heart to the sound of God's voice in your heart. Listen and expect, and even if you don't hear clear words you will feel God moving deep inside you ready to release faith-inspired words of healing and breakthrough into your situation.

You see, this is high impact praying and it always leads to high impact results. You can take something simple to begin building your faith. You may have a simple need that you want to be met. Start there, and begin to concentrate your thoughts on the reality of heaven inside. Then when you feel the release, call those things that be not as though they were. Once you've prayed it, settle that it is done in your heart and release expectation for your harvest to come.

I remember a time when this principle of prayer really impacted my life. I was going to visit my mother in a transition home as she was recovering from some recent injuries. On my way to the transition facility I had to pass through the nursing home part of the building to see her. Every day I passed through, there was a woman in the living area who would look at me with this look of great frustration. She was a sweet elderly lady with beautiful curly red hair.

Soon, I realized that the source of her frustration was that she couldn't speak. She was mute and her frustration was coming from her trying to talk.

For about a week and half, day after day this woman would be in the living area frustrating herself trying to speak. She would look at me and I would think to myself, *"Lord bless this woman."* One day as I was entering the building, God put it in my heart to pray for this woman. He reminded to concentrate on His power within me and to channel that energy and authority with my words.

Now, when I got there I didn't see her so I began to head to the other side of the facility to see my mother. Suddenly, I felt someone grab my shirt from behind. It was the lady with the beautiful red hair! She was really frustrated trying to get my attention as the nurses watched nearby. All of a sudden that same power I felt entering the building rose back up in my spirit and with a faith-infused declaration I touched the side of her face and said, "Lord, let this woman's mouth be opened that she may speak clearly."

Nothing happened at first, but I began to admire her hair as I rubbed it and started having a conversation with her as if she was already talking back.

Within a few minutes, she suddenly opened her mouth and said, "Do you like my hair?" She said, "Everyone is always complimenting my hair but I can never respond." I could see great joy overwhelming her as we talked.

I laughed at her words and the nurses that we were watching were filled with great excitement. They shared that the woman had been there for nearly 10 years and never spoken a clear word. I believe that day I discovered a powerful principle that I am trying to share with you now. By concentrating on the God in me and not my own ability, I was able to channel His power through my words and accomplish God's will for this woman in the earth.

It's time to expect God to infuse you with high impact prayers. Focus your thoughts on heaven's authority within you and realize that wordiness is not necessary when praying with this pursuit. You are strapped with spiritual dynamite. And you are about to release the God-life in you through the power of high impact praying.

The Internal Power of Navigation

As you draw more and more from this Kingdom authority of high impact prayer, it's no longer just you praying, but God's spirit through you acting as an internal force inspiring your heart with spirit-charged words to speak into your own life or even petition on someone else's behalf. You are destined to win once you realize the power of God's internal compass that can lead you into victory without any limitations. I want to encourage you to tell God: *"You are my guide, and my internal navigator. Charge my heart with the Word and unleash heavenly access through me."*

I think Psalm 119:105 paints the perfect picture:

Your word is a lamp for my feet, a light on my path.

It's important that we realize the more we focus on the Word (light) within us, which is the ability and life flow of God in our spirit, the more we are able to charge our thoughts with the truth of God's presence flowing in us. This will give us the power we need to speak life to everything and every situation. Our words are supercharged with Kingdom authority when we access this realm of imaginative thinking. The internal paradigm of the Creator within us is the source of His internal navigation.

God wants to influence our approach to praying with a more authoritative stance based on His internal government inside of us. So, His light again refers to the influence of the Kingdom. The same way we were translated from the kingdom of darkness into the Kingdom of light (sound), we now have the ability to influence the atmosphere with power words charged by power thoughts as navigated by the inspired will of God's internal compass.

Let God's thoughts inspire your heart and direct your words with powerful petition. As you do, I can guarantee you will notice a whole new you praying with the force of heaven as you release simple and short, yet powerful petitions. In doing so you'll further unleash the rule of God's Kingdom into greater jurisdiction in your life and the world around you.

Power Concepts from this Chapter

❖ God has restored us back to our original position in the Kingdom as divine beings with all provision met spiritually and materially.

❖ Our provision comes through divine revelation of where His solution rests, where the harvest is, and His strategy for reaping that harvest now.

❖ Our boldness should flow from our understanding of who we really are in the Kingdom, that we are co-heirs with Christ reigning in His government now.

❖ Pray from the posture of a winning position rather than the defeated perspective of a losing seat.

❖ If we are going to learn how to continually draw from the wellspring of divine life within us, there has to be a commitment to take a faith stand against every negative fear-based way of thinking and speaking.

❖ Mindsets of negativity and opposition are constantly trying to gain ground in our lives so that we will continually to be ruled by another language and kept out of our inheritance.

The Power of Sound: Understanding the Laws of Kingdom Language

4

The Law of Sound

Gaining perception of God's will is only effective when we are able to communicate that same will in the earth. In doing so, spiritually speaking, we are now "matching tones" with God and making His sound. The core purpose of learning to tap into God's frequency sound is not simply to receive revelation; it's taking what God is actually saying and communicating that same exact sound in the earth realm.

You know, the entire purpose of God giving us His Word is to enable to us to line up with His communication system. The system of prayer was never designed for us to take on the burden of self-effort, nor was it designed for us to assume the role of determining what to pray. If you examine the Bible closely, it is clear that communication in the Kingdom was always designed to depend on something God has already said. For example, Romans 8:26 is clear that we don't know what we should be praying, however the Spirit within us can accurately interpret God's will and translate that to us through His Kingdom in our spirit.

Mistakenly, common belief systems about effective prayer place the responsibility of knowing what to pray on the one who prays. And many tend to only take the paradigm of prayer as something we do rather than something we live. That is not accurate. Prayer is a spiritual order that functions continuously, whether we are aware of it or not.

Consequently, a common frustration of unanswered prayer seems to plague the spiritual walks of many. I believe it's simply because most haven't been taught how to operate the laws of prayer effectively or how to live in them. It remains vital then that we understand prayer is not designed for us to make deposits to God; it is intended for us to make withdrawals from Him. Once we receive from Him first then agreeing in faith we should release God's Word or promise to us as spiritual seed into our atmosphere and life. Now this is a bit of a paradigm shift concerning the view most people take about prayer. However, we are called *the bride* (of Christ), which then puts us on the receiving end of things concerning our intimate encounters with God. Essentially, we are spiritual incubators and God is our husbandman, so we should always approach prayer with a receiving mindset rather than depositing one.

That is why Revelation 22:17 indicates clearly that the resounding chant within the spirit of Christ's bride says, "Come." Again, the understanding of being His bride puts us on the receiving end, not a depositing one. We have to understand that God is our progenitor and has programmed us through His Kingdom to receive, discern, correctly interpret, and then reproduce His will in planet earth.

He is always waiting to inject us with the spiritual seed of revelation that can clearly show us what to say, how to pray, and the strategy for releasing Blessing. This was always the original function of prayer, and until individuals discover the Kingdom paradigm of praying, which is perceiving, receiving and then simply releasing God's sound in the earth, they will continue in frustration of inconsistency in their overall communication with God in His Kingdom.

Once we master this simple and basic principle about Kingdom prayer, many things in our lives will begin to line up with the frequency levels of heaven, and we will watch as things conform to exactly what we've said as we speak God's will into our lives. Quite simply, your effectiveness in prayer lies in your ability to say exactly what God is saying in heaven about your situation and then to release that into the earth. Nevertheless, this can be easier said than done.

Sound, by definition, refers to energy waves that travel or transmit themselves through frequencies within the range of hearing. All energy travels by waves and waves travel by patterns. Energy travels in wavelengths. When waves connect they create patterns that can carry on for miles. In fact, energy waves are so powerful that depending on the force; an earthquake in California can be felt in Africa. When you see waves in an ocean current, those waves are only passing through the top of the water, because frequencies travel through the surface of things.

Similarly, when God created man He used the highest ranges of frequency to match His sound and produce an image that reflected His exact likeness. In other words, man was streamlined with God's very heart and intention to produce His exact image and likeness in the earth realm. What's even more interesting is that the word *image* in the Hebrew comes from the word *pattern*. Remember that when waves connect they create patterns.

So, man is the image, or pattern, created by the connecting points of God's frequency waves with ours. This is important to understand because where the Bible mentions instruments and music the emphasis is really about God's *sound*. When it talks about light in reference to darkness, it is painting a picture of God's Kingdom and its frequency versus the frequency of Babylon. In

Genesis 1, the writer is very clear when he dictates that darkness was on the face of the deep.

Here God is painting a picture that the satanic kingdom was in authority at this point. When God said, "Let there be light," He translated His frequency into the earth, and through those patterns He shaped mankind as a sort of "wavelength" of His Word. Thus His genius and authority ripples throughout all of creation and with the greatest parts of His genetic build residing in the human being. What this means for you and I is that your ability to engage the Kingdom of heaven and bring God's will into earth through sound communication depends on your ability to line up with this truth or sound. Your creation is literally the reflection of the very wave pattern of God's intention.

Within your genetic make-up is the DNA of the King and the divine ability to translate heaven into earth if you will agree with the creative sound or intention in you and the purpose He is communicating to you through His will right now. Nevertheless, the purpose of these patterns and wavelengths that carry sound are to produce hearing. Again, when I say hearing I mean "perception." You see the Kingdom of God altogether is a subconscious and spiritual force that manifests itself through God's creative perceptions and internal paradigm lens within our heart. It's His outlook on life and His way of doing things.

By intentionally tapping into His sound you are able to create the right *perception* about your life. Now you can see or perceive wisdom and revelation that will ultimately guide you into the harvest you have been praying for. You see, God is a spirit and His Kingdom is spiritual. By truly grasping these principles you will come into the understanding of how God's Spirit in you operates His perception to draw from.

Nothing God wants to do in your life can happen until it comes by perception. This world's system, however, wants you to change radars and bow your thoughts to a concept of life that is objective rather than subjective. It wants you to think carnally, which will eventually shape the wrong perception about what God is doing in you. It wants you to live limited, think defeated, and to operate beneath your potential as a royal citizen in the Kingdom of God.

But you have the Kingdom within you, which means you possess everything you need to enforce God's tangible will for your life today. As you perceive His Word and gain His perspective of your life you will begin aligning your words, thoughts and actions with what He is saying. This explains why Jesus was able to experience such incredible results with His ministry while on earth. In John 5 He explains that His being able to "see and hear" what God was doing and saying was the cause of His success. This is the heart of the Kingdom paradigm of praying. This is how we access 100% effective results with praying. By tuning into God's perception and drawing from it to know what God is saying and doing and only speaking and obeying that. If you do this, the outward expression of tangible blessing will be sure to overtake you and take you to another level.

So, the principle concerning the law of sound is simple: As you agree with God and begin to tap into His perfect will, you'll activate His paradigm lens or perception. This is the place from which the door of all tangible Kingdom manifestation will emerge. From there you will begin leveraging those accurate spiritual perceptions to boldly communicate the will of God into any area of your life. As a result the tangible life-flow of His will must translate and channel its authority through your bold confession as a mandate to produce outward tangible manifestation of the influence and authenticity of God's Kingdom operating in your life. This is how you operate the Kingdom of God effectively through the divine communication system of heaven, the law of prayer.

Streamlining Communication

As God's sound continually increases within, you should gradually become conformed to His way of life. Again, the purpose of that sound is to create the right perception, and based on that perception we can speak the very heart of God as authoritative influence into our physical life. In other words, the power of God's sound living in us should translate into unstoppable power we live out everyday. God's sound becomes our language, a powerful force that can produce anything we desire to see happening in our lives.

Now, when I say language I am referring to the things we are saying all the time. We express language through much more than our petitions to God. Whether you realize it or not, our language is one of the defining characteristics that determine what kingdom is prevalent and operating in our life. This is because language stands as one of the three main cultural blocks of kingdom influence.

The other two major cultural blocks are value and philosophy. When a Kingdom wants to expand its territory and subdue new land, it takes over an area that becomes known as a "province." A province is simply territory that is a part of a country outside of its capital or the largest cities. When God sees planet earth He sees in a sense, a potential province of heaven, and His desire and intent is to influence this country or province with His values, language and philosophy. The purpose of this is so that earth becomes more like the Kingdom culture of heaven. So, language is a powerful force of influence that can create and expand heavenly authority into the earth realm.

In order for God's language to influence earth, He needs a representative to declare and speak on His behalf. This is where you and I come in. We are heaven's ambassadors charged with the assignment of increasing the Kingdom of God in the earth through the main cultural blocks of influence. The more we demonstrate

God's language and culture, the more the earth will know what He looks like.

The conflict we are faced with as divine diplomats is the culture and influence of the Babylonian kingdom in this world. Every day, through different outlets and sources, the Satanic kingdom is trying to influence our language, values, and belief systems. It's up to us to determine to continue engaging God as our only source and depend upon His sound to give us freedom from the reigns of earthly world empires by giving us the right perception to speak the right things constantly.

Streamlining is our answer to every attack of miscommunication in this world. When I say streamline, I am referring to one's ability to tap into the constant stream of God's thoughts that are flowing within us and repeat those same thoughts as word power into the earth. You see, God isn't looking for "prayer experts." He isn't looking for people who speak in tongues the most for the fastest or the longest. He isn't looking for individuals with the greatest track record, background or spiritual experience. God simply wants people who are willing to position themselves to receive from Him. Remember God said that *He* knows His plans for us. And if our prosperity is tied to God's plan and that plan must be communicated in the earth, God is only concerned with streamlining His heart for us to advance good things into our lives. In other words, God wants listeners rather than talkers.

I love to refer to Mary concerning this principal as she performed one of the greatest miracles in the Bible with one simple prayer: *"At your Word let it be unto me as you've spoken."* By learning to communicate God's will following this simple high impact model of praying she became pregnant as a virgin with the living Son of God. Her words released the will of God that the angel streamlined to her. In other words she simply said what God said!

Notice that nowhere in the passage does it say that Mary was in the "act of" praying when the angel approached her. It doesn't mention a fast or any type of self-effort on her behalf. She was simply positioned spiritually to receive because she had streamline communication with God. This is how the law of prayer should operate in every Christian's life. By becoming a receiver she then "received" something that changed her life and the world.

This may sound simple but it is a core process to how Kingdom communication functions. Young Mary provides a consistent model for all Kingdom citizens to follow. Here we gain those powerful results with praying by adjusting our angle of pursuit and repositioning ourselves for total agreement with something God has already said. God, who reigns in the country called heaven, simply needs a human being for spiritual diplomacy to believe Him and declare His words so that He can influence and transform the province called earth into a colony of heaven.

In a practical sense, prayer becomes the system for communicating our government's policy into the earth realm in order to influence this life. So, at the heart of streamlining God's thoughts is the power of agreement. When we choose to agree with the King's policy (something He's already said), we are then likely to become determined to see His perfect will communicated in the earth through ourselves as heavenly agents, representative, and ambassadors.

God's Divine Plan of Diplomacy

Though this may challenge some traditional views you've probably had concerning the meaning of prayer and how it functions, by adapting to this Kingdom insight about prayer you are better positioned to really make an impact in the earth with the Kingdom of God. Prayer is your divine plan to succeed and ensure total victory over every obstacle. The totality of the Blessing and all inheritance we receive in Christ finds its culmination in the communication system of prayer. Prayer is designed to empower your spirit with utter confidence that what you've said is actually coming to pass because you are speaking God's will.

Knowing this helps you gain a better understanding of God's overall purpose and plan for placing mankind in the earth. In Genesis 1 and 2 we witness God's government plan of deployment through the first royal diplomat known to man named Adam.

Adam, under the direction and authority of the Holy Spirit (the Chief Ambassador), is commanded by God (the King) to take dominion over the land. Essentially, God was explaining Adam's mission plainly but also revealing to all of mankind His powerful intent and purpose for us as earthly residents. He wants to us to rule with mastery and excellence just by simply leveraging our direct and unlimited access to His will and communication system to influence the earth with it. That's right, all of this clear and uninterrupted communication between God and Adam is taking place within Adam's spirit. God's *sound,* as Genesis 3 gives insight to, is Adam's source of fellowship with God in the Garden.

Adam's streamlined communication with God was the elemental force to his success. What God wants you to understand is that same communication has been restored through Christ. Now you can resume that same accurate communication with Him and live empowered with total victory through correctly aligned Kingdom praying. If you will really set your hearts to believing this powerful Kingdom agenda, God will streamline to your heart from heaven like never before. Your accurate perception and declaration of His will is what reunites you with the purpose of God's heart in the earth through divine diplomacy.

I challenge you to really embrace and take to heart the concept of Kingdom diplomacy. Allow yourself to truly draw from the inner picture of your power seat and position of influence in the Kingdom.

The Blessing of Diplomacy

So, what is God's will for us? What is His ultimate plan? It is to prosper us without limits through His government within us that others may be inspired to pursue His purpose for their lives as well. When we communicate correctly with our divine headquarters, we're empowering ourselves to do just that, thrive and excel without limits. So it's clear to see that God's plan has always revolved around foreign diplomacy. Diplomacy simply describes the skillful conduct in the art and science of international relations. In the United States we refer to our foreign agents as diplomats or ambassadors who operate under the authority of the "secretary of state," who is the head of all international affairs.

In spiritual regards, you are divinely employed by the Kingdom of heaven to perform skillful international influence under the authority of our "secretary of state", the Holy Spirit. Understanding divine diplomacy sets the pathway for powerful and successful praying because real diplomats are never inspired of their own will; everything they do, say, and produce is inspired by the will of their king or leader who has sent them. In our case, we should continually be inspired by the will of Him who put us here on earth. Our prayers should be driven by an intense desire to see our King's plan manifested through us. This is how the Kingdom comes alive within you: when the same thing that drives God becomes the same thing that drives you.

When we operate in a diplomatic state of mind, we can prepare for greater outcomes when we release petitions to God, knowing all provision is met by our government. We can also be confident in hearing God's sound (voice), knowing that He always has an assignment for us to prosper and increase His foreign policy plan in the earth.

So, you have not only been employed but you have also been deployed. And your understanding of both will have a lasting effect on how you pray, your mindset when praying, and your overall expectation to receive exactly what you asked. You have to position yourself with the correct understanding of foreign influence through God's will.

> *For this reason, since the day we heard of you we have not stopped praying for you and asking God to fill you with the knowledge of His will through all spiritual wisdom and understanding.*

> Colossians 1:9 (AMP)

Power Concepts from this Chapter

❖ God wants us to take what He is saying and communicate that same exact sound into the earth realm.

❖ The entire purpose of God giving us His Word is to enable to us to line up with His communication system.

❖ You have the Kingdom within you and you possess everything you need to tap into the sound of God.

❖ As you agree with God's nature (sound) in you, it will activate His perception, or internal paradigm, which emerges as a subconscious force called the Kingdom of God.

❖ God's language is a powerful force of influence that can create and expand heavenly authority into the earth realm.

❖ The more we demonstrate God's language and culture, the more the earth will know what He looks like.

❖ It's up to us to determine to continue to engage God as our source and depend upon His sound to give us the right perception to speak the right things.

Empowering Your Life: Supercharging Your Atmosphere

5

The Concept of Life and Death

When Adam chose to accept the idea that he was not made in the likeness and image of God, he opened the door to a whole new system of thinking to govern his life with. And since thoughts are the power source of what we say, Adam naturally began to change his language from the communication system of *life* to the communication system of the earth cursed kingdom called *death*.

Once Adam changed languages he literally gave permission to what had been cultivating within his thoughts to tangibly exist in an outward expression. This is because our mouth is the birth canal of our thoughts. Those ideas and concepts that we believe in adopt and form relationships with our minds. When those thoughts are spoken out loud they are given legal access to manifest. So, what you're thinking is most certainly alive, but what you say allows it to take shape.

Once we meditate on one single idea the process of conception begins and eventually what we have conceived will take birth in our words. However, we must remember that what we say is only the result of things we have truly believed deep within our hearts and through constant entertainment and interaction with those belief systems we give birth to concepts or principles that govern our entire state of living.

In the same sense, God is clear that His language is solely based on the concept of *life*. And the things of this world, governed by Satan's kingdom, find their source in the concept called *death*. Death reigns in the earth through mindsets that have been charged with belief systems that oppose the Kingdom of God. Life is the mark of truth, which as I mentioned previously, is the highest reality. That reality is the reality of heaven reigning in the spiritual world as the dominant kingdom.

God's language of life is simply charged by the principles that rule His government. Those principles flow from God's heart, as He is the King and wishes to express those same ideas through the lives of His representatives in the earth realm. It is important to point out that every Kingdom is ruled by the thoughts and ideas of its King.

So the King's plan then, is to teach His citizens His language model called *life*, but only by endowing them with the source of His thoughts based solely off His supreme reality called truth. That is why I keep saying the Kingdom of God is an internal paradigm. Yes, it is a real government ruled by Jesus who is King. It is also an outward expression of an internal position in one's heart. This position in one's heart becomes the governing seat that Jesus then rules from.

Again, how that Kingdom shows up in our life is through concepts that rule our thoughts. Those concepts determine our paradigm. That paradigm determines what kingdom is ruling in our lives. That is how God gets His Kingdom over to His royal representatives living in the earth: through concepts of life.

He wants to govern our life by shaping our thoughts with concepts that reflect His will, priorities and original design for us. In the same token, the ruler of this world's kingdom is eager to influence our mindsets with his approach to life called death. Death really just describes any system outside of God's way of doing things. The Hebrew meaning of the word literally references detachment from God. Death again, is simply a sound, just as light is; however, it is an opposing sound to heaven's Kingdom. This cursed world kingdom transmits its sound waves as thoughts and imaginations that inspire ideas and belief systems in individuals that are not empowered by God's heart. The purpose is to then produce that sound in the earth through words to accomplish an assignment completely opposite of God's motives.

It simply trains individuals to operate in a Babylonian system, which is a world outside of God's intentional design for us ruled with concepts of fear, lies, and doubt. When these sounds are continually active in one's life, a revolving door and endless cycle repeat themselves and unfavorable conditions continue to rule in the lives of God's people. You were made for more than that.

That is why it so imperative that we become familiar with how kingdoms function. Remember, the mouth is the birth canal of our thoughts and it gives ideas permission to exist as outward expressions of sound that will determine what we attract and what we become.

The Uprising of Death's Language

We first see the language of death active through mankind after Adam's fall from his power seat in the Kingdom of God. Look at these scripture verses in Genesis 3:8-10.

> *Then the man and his wife heard the sound of the LORD God as he was walking in the garden in the cool of the day, and they hid from the LORD God among the trees of the garden. But the LORD God called to the man, "Where are you?" He answered, "I heard you in the garden, and I was afraid because I was naked; so I hid."*

Several important things are happening in these verses. Firstly, Adam is speaking with a new language system inspired by another kingdom. His confession of himself has changed from being like God to being *naked and afraid*. Here the concept of abandonment is presented. So when he says he is afraid, he is like a child alone without a father feeling as though he has no place to call home.

Although God didn't abandon Adam, his self-conscious limitations have impacted his belief systems so much that he is now afraid of God and has decided to operate in a kingdom outside of God. Now clearly by this passage we can see that God isn't angry with Adam at all. Furthermore, Adam is still on the same wavelength and communication stream as God too. That is why the passage mentions that Adam and Eve "heard the sound of the Lord."

Now here again is the concept of sound being presented as the major force that expresses God's presence. So if Adam and Eve heard God's sound, they were still in communication with Him operating the language system of prayer. However, Babylon had begun to dominate Adam's vocabulary, which is evident in his negative confession of himself. Now look at what happens next in verse 11:

> *And he said, "Who told you that you were naked? Have you eaten from the tree that I commanded you not to eat from?*

Realizing this was not the language God had taught Adam, He inquired as to where he learned this new type of communication. Since only one other kingdom could possibly influence Adam's thoughts and environment God immediately points out that Adam has eaten from the tree of the knowledge of *good and evil*. This is mixed fruit. The tree represents a reproductive system, which is a kingdom and culture. Just like the female takes in seed from the male, undergoes the process of conception and eventually gives birth to a new life, in the same fashion, the tree is indicative of a reproductive system and force: the kingdom of darkness.

Since the tree is full of *knowledge* it contains *concepts*. Those concepts possess seed from the progenitor, or the one who planted it. So anyone who takes in those concepts becomes impregnated with the same seed and reproduces that same system of concept or thought. This is what happens to Adam when he eats or takes on a new philosophy that doesn't line up with God's word. Although the tree appears to be good up-close or after a personal encounter, it gives birth to unfruitful things.

So, what I am saying is the tree represents the process of how we take in ideas and concepts, conceive them, and then eventually give birth to them through the birth canal of our words. Adam's experience models the perfect example of how Christians continually become influenced through sound by the cursed world kingdom although they have the ability to tap into God's sound and frequency now. Like Adam, this power still exists for us all.

You see, Adam never lost the ability to hear God's sound; he chose not to operate in it. That means he chose another kingdom. Remember that hearing is perception that produces the substance of our thoughts.

The Consistency of Life

In essence, as Kingdom citizens every believer has the ability to tap into God's sound. It wasn't until Adam made that confession of himself that God was forced to turn him over to the kingdom called "the curse", because that was the major source of his language, value and philosophical cultural systems. Basically, by changing sounds Adam had changed kingdoms. By his own will, Adam wasn't speaking life anymore. Rather, he was agreeing with his circumstances and speaking out of alignment with heavenly communication.

We have to learn the importance of always speaking life to all things to all people at all times. This language determines what government is ruling in our lives. You really should take a moment to examine: what language am I speaking all the time? You see, life is a communication system called prayer. It doesn't shut off when we stop "praying." It's always active just like any spiritual or natural law. That means what you are saying at work and at home all day long is directly linked to the impact your words will have when you try to speak over other situations.

You must understand that the spiritual laws of the universe don't operate based on situations. These laws are solely based on communication, as in what you are saying all the time. You absolutely cannot expect real results with prayer if you aren't always speaking in the streamline of Kingdom communication.

Heaven's thoughts and words have to continually be flowing in order for there to be true agreement with the system of heavenly communication called prayer. As you gain a clearer picture of this reality, you begin to really see that the power of the tongue is the source of our birth canals, our mouth.

The sad truth is that many people have not grasped this understanding. They think prayer ends when they are through making requests to God or praying in spiritual tongues. This is far from the truth. Once you make petition to God about a matter, the spiritual laws of the universe are waiting to see what you say about that situation all the time and what you're speaking about everything else. Many people make powerful supplications to God. But when seemingly unfavorable events arise they abort heavenly communication and say what they feel.

And this seemingly small act can potentially wipe out the legitimacy of what they just asked for in prayer and petition (in God's language). This may seem like a small matter in our eyes.

However, spiritually it's like jumping back and forth between two different lines of communication. This imbalance and confusion will not produce consistent results, only frustrating ones.

In other circumstances, someone can make sound supplications to God concerning their present conditions. However, there may be un-forgiveness in their heart toward someone and later that day they are slandering that individual without even realizing it. Well, believe it or not this is why Jesus tells us to forgive before we pray. He literally links forgiveness and asking together. Why? Because Jesus is clearly expressing to us that what we say about others has a direct impact on our prayer effectiveness. I am telling you that if believers will get this principle down in their hearts they will realize some major sources of unanswered prayer.

You will lose your prayer power if you don't manage how you speak all the time about everyone. This is a hidden truth that Jesus taught about prayer, speaking God's language all the time. And though it has been rarely taught, this law of Kingdom communication bears a weight of truth that, when accessed and applied, will change your experience with prayer forever.

Avoiding Pitfalls of Bad Communication

It's obvious that the most prevalent consequence of misaligned praying is unanswered prayer. And again, as much it has been taught to us that God listens to every prayer, on the basis of sound biblical principle, that simply is not the truth. In order to gain better results with praying in the Kingdom, we have to be careful to move beyond emotions and feelings based on what we've always heard to a true desirous pursuit of accurate Kingdom truth. In other words, must pray correctly!

In John 8:32, Jesus said that when we know that truth we'll be set free. Or, as I like to put it: *when we learn the truth about what we are really facing, we can change what we are doing wrong and begin experiencing winning outcomes.* There is plenty of scriptural evidence that proves it is possible to pray wrong (i.e. Matthew 6:14, James 4:3). Prayer is the official language of Kingdom citizens and when we don't operate those laws of language correctly, God, many times, will not respond.

Think about this, if God listened and responded to incorrect prayer, what would be the measuring tool to keep us from praying wrongly? Understanding the law of prayer and how it functions requires some undoing of things we've learned along the way that haven't been right. It is also a call to spiritual maturity because the foundation of prosperity in the Kingdom is seasoned ripeness (Psalm 1:1-3 AMP). This is one's ability to adapt to new truth and apply that truth while moving beyond old belief systems that haven't been very fruitful. So, if we are going to avoid one of the major pitfalls of misaligned prayer we have to be prepared to come into a mature understanding of how this system functions.

The result of bad communication is not always unanswered prayer. However, many times the consequence shows up as delay. And some of those delays can be so drawn out that it feels as though our prayers will never be answered. Have you ever felt as though some prayers that should have been answered were being delayed? You may be able to relate to the feeling of exhaustion and exasperation that comes from extreme delay. Sometimes we need to go back and make the right confession over our situation and determine to stay in agreement with the language of life. If we will submit our heart to God, He will show us things we are saying, thinking and holding onto that interrupt our communication signal to heaven.

When we change our mindsets we regain a clear picture of the Kingdom authority within us as we can clearly hear the King's voice again telling us what to say. Consequently, we can once again clearly transmit God's heart into the earth over our situations. Our heart then becomes bolder as power charged petitions begin to spring forth with expectation of immediate results. It's possible to get the results you have always desired with powerful prayer. However, understanding the concept of life's language and the concept of the language of death will give you greater clarity of how to manage your thoughts and ideas and examine what's inspiring them. You'll begin to become a master of thoughts as well as a steward of your words.

Words are one of your most powerful resources, and they are the tangible substance of your thoughts. Whether we are aware of it or not, the language laws of creation are always in perpetuation and the language we use the most is going to determine if, when, or how long it is before our answers manifest. Always remember that as Kingdom citizens, heaven is readily accessible through its sound. Also, remain conscious that your citizenship permits you with the authority to eliminate those barriers and pitfalls of unanswered prayer with sound communication.

Transmitting Your Power Seat through Prayer

I want you to understand that when you come into maturity of your prayer language called *life* you are literally empowering your life. You are creating new opportunities for tangible releases of heavenly influence by cultivating the atmosphere. Recalling Adam's encounter with *death*, he certainly took on a new language and culture. He was transmitting a new sound wave or signal that didn't correspond with the frequency of heaven.

Again, when this happened he literally changed Kingdoms. Likewise within us all is the same ability to either transmit Kingdom communication or, through the changing of thoughts, we can perpetuate the sound of another kingdom. That's why it's important to understand our translation from the kingdom of darkness to the Kingdom of Light. You have changed over from one kingdom of sound (death) to another Kingdom of superior sound (life).

As I mentioned previously, that change happened in your spirit, which is what you are: a spirit being. God created then formed you from the sound of clear communication through His voice, which is the Word. So, by transmitting His wavelength into the earth realm your entire spirit being was shaped in God's image, which is the visual reflection of His sound and energy. Christ, who is the Word, redeemed us from the fall of Adam and restored our communication rights with God by empowering us through His Kingdom of Grace. Now every believer, as citizens of heaven, can enforce God's sound through their words, overpowering every obstacle and challenge with the supreme transmission of a superior frequency and sound, the Kingdom of Light. You are redeemed; Eden has been restored to you within your spirit and you are complete, whole and positioned in the power seat of authority and success. Your prosperity in this earth realm is simply a matter of you understanding how to channel God's thoughts to produce His sound waves. And through the birth canal of your mouth you transmit powerful frequencies that will release heaven's atmosphere in the earth and over your life.

You see that is what Eden is, a spiritual atmosphere created by the sound waves of heaven. It's the extension of God's Kingdom of Light into another realm or territory of influence. In other words, you are about to tap into the power to translate God's Kingdom into the earth through supercharged atmospheres produced by your words. Believe it or not, this is the source of Kingdom praying and how the language system of heaven operates on consistent and supreme levels. It's time to leverage the laws of prayer and kingdom communication to create an atmosphere of supercharged energy that will transmit your spiritual authority into a material seat or power position of influence and advantage in this world.

Supercharge Your Atmosphere

As I said before you are a divine being created from the most powerful wavelength of energy: the Word of God! This energy doesn't begin in our physical life; it starts with our spirit man, our souls, and then our bodies. Let's look at how our spiritual energy can help create and shape the environment needed to escape chaos and produce conducive and healthy living conditions for successful spiritual living. In terms of praying, we further examine the atmospheric impact of speaking words charged with heavenly communication.

Referencing back to Genesis 1 we find that the world and all creation, including humans, sprang forth from the life-giving energy of God's Word. The moment God said let there be light His tangible energy was released in the earth giving all creation the ability to produce magnetic energy fields of their own. In fact, John 1 refers to the Word as light, which is simply energy. As energetic beings we have flowing through us positive and negative protons that are creating invisible fields that we live under.

Our sphere of influence or "garden" is made up of this energy, whether negative or positive. Whatever we release in our thoughts and words literally create energy fields that will draw things to us based on the energy we exude and release. The positive energy flows from the Kingdom of God, God's nature, and His system of sound within us. Negative energy flows from the fallen nature in every man, which is powered by the kingdom of darkness. The great news is that we have the ability to choose what field we will live in based on our words, philosophies, and even the relationships we entertain. This field will determine our destiny, as the energy of who we are will ultimately release and attract to us what we have invested into our outer spheres.

A good example is when Elijah prayed for rain (1 Kings 18). He was charging the atmosphere, waiting for a release because it was due. It was simple supernatural law; he created a field or cloud of tension and the discharge was due because of his simultaneous declarations.

The "garden" is a spiritual atmosphere created when the right things are continually spoken into the same place. God consistently, for seven days, spoke into one spot in the earth and created a magnetic field with a supercharged atmosphere called "Eden." The Kingdom of heaven is a spiritual diameter and an invisible magnet that is only effective if we are charging it with the right things. That's why whatever you sow comes right back to you. Your field is generating a discharge. If you say, "I'm sick of my job" enough times, you'll eventually get sick or you'll notice conflict emerging with the boss and now more and more problems arise, because you kept charging your atmosphere with those atoms.

In the same way, when the right frequencies are transmitted into the right place, over time they will eventually make room for new energy. When this happens a discharge occurs and draws exactly to you the charges you have released through thoughts and words.

A discharge is a release of tension and energy. We see this with lightning and thunder. Once the stress or tension of energy in the sky reaches a breaking point, the clouds release a discharge in the physical form of lighting and the audible sound of thunder. This is why the Bible says He appears in a "cloud" of glory and thunder and lightning are surrounding Him. These are all illustrations and displays of how His Kingdom operates.

What do you say the most? That's what is happening to you. Faith is the "substance" of what is hoped for. That means its material substance is produced by an expectation for something. "Sub" means under, and "stance" means to stand. It's literally standing ground; that's an atmosphere or reality. You are creating the ground you walk on and the reality you live in with your words. So if your faith is the spiritual substance of what you're expecting, your words become that spiritual substance causing that thing to tangibly take form through the energy of words being released into the atmosphere. When you put a seed in the ground a crop grows. That's the easy part. And as long as it is cultivated and properly watered it will produce a crop. That's your atmosphere. When you speak words, you sow into your future and what you have said will soon enough discharge and a harvest will come forth.

I love what Joel Osteen says: "If you want to see what someone's life will be like 5 years from now just listen to what they are saying about themselves now." That is the power of charging your atmosphere, and the more conscious of this you become the more powerful you'll become as a Kingdom citizen expressing your spiritual authority in tangible forms.

Now, I want to be clear that this spiritual principle has spiritual laws attached that govern it like any other Kingdom model. For example, If you declare, "I am wealthy" enough it doesn't necessarily mean money will appear the next day. However you will release ideas and strategies that can make you wealthy because that is what you've sown into your atmosphere. All of the characteristics, qualities, habits, and connections you need to become wealthy will begin to flow to you because of the discharge you have created in your spiritual garden. If you are willing to apply those strategies and take action, you will inevitably begin tapping into your wealthy place.

The Empowered You

Remember that our lives are controlled by what we always do. The more you realize that with every word you are charging an invisible field that will eventually attract the same energy back to you, you'll gain a clearer picture and greater understanding of the God nature that's in you.

As a kingdom citizen you are never in a season so bad that you can't shift the atmosphere and begin to create change. If you are always speaking life, God promises that's what is going to show up. That is how we keep negativity out of our lives by keeping life on our tongues.

It's important to remember you are the Word. All those 75 trillion cells in your body are the result of magnetic impulses from God's mouth. You were literally formed in God's image or field so that you could begin attracting all His characteristics. Don't underestimate the power of one word. Don't underestimate the power of what's in you. There are great things coming forth because you are shifting the atmospheres of your life, relationships, and finances. Change the atmosphere through laws of faith and Kingdom paradigm praying. There may be a negative contract you need to specifically verbalize and break up with. Have faith and speak life to what you have spoken death to. Because the resurrection power that raised Jesus was the Word and that same Word is in your mouth to raise back to life the things you have spoken death to consistently.

What's in Your Atmosphere?

It is without doubt that most people have created negative fields. They have believed a negative concept, idea, or philosophy for so long they've created a spiritual field that only yields that harvest. Some confess but see no results. They declare but don't actually see what they have said come to pass. Why? It isn't because they don't possess the God-given potential to produce results with prayer. It's because some of us have created toxic spiritual fields that can only be broken by the power of the right words being constantly spoken into the atmosphere.

We have to change our atmosphere by changing our words; however, changing our words and speaking the right things continually takes commitment, discipline, and follow through. These are the traits of true Kingdom citizenship.

For so long I struggled with depression and a pessimistic view of life. I couldn't seem to get ahead and it seemed like doors were always closing on me. I used to think to myself, "Man, I sure have the worst luck." Actually I was right! As a result, that's what kept on producing in my life and atmosphere.

My breakthrough came when I decided that just maybe the way I am thinking and speaking could be influencing this perpetual negative cycle. So I decided to change my thoughts and my words. For 90 days straight I focused on disciplining healthy, positive, life-generating thoughts and positively charged words. I decided it was my life and no one was responsible for it but me and I have the power to change things. I quickly noticed that when I changed my perception about certain things, right along with it followed the kind of confession I was making. I began to see that things in my life were exactly how I said they were because I believed it. Therefore, what I believed I became. I wasn't using my citizenship authority very much and as a result of this, I was missing out on the tremendous benefits of Eden's provision package lying dormant inside my spirit.

One of the ways we release the material benefits is through Kingdom communication and the law of prayer. So, I began to see my energy field created by thoughts, imaginations, and words. I had to break that negative field I caused through deceptive mentalities and negative fear-filled words. Turns out, I wasn't speaking heaven's language consistently. As a result, my prayer success was very inconsistent and ineffective. Truthfully, it didn't happen overnight, and in some cases I had to make the right confession for 60 to 90 days straight in order to see breakthrough in particular areas of my life. As I have experienced, there are many of us who have said the wrong things for so long that the words we use aren't powerful enough to break that atmosphere immediately.

You have to choose to say the right things consistently around the clock, owning your day with supercharged and faith-filled words. Doing this will eventually move out those negative electrons in your atmosphere you need in order to experience and attract God's best for you. I believe the Kingdom of heaven shows up as an intangible energy field and force that, when yielded to, will produce the reality of God's most favorable conditions in your life.

Apostle Paul briefly shared about this experience by saying that if we keep our minds above the earth, heaven's atmosphere will explode into our physical reality (Colossians 3). He encouraged us that our minds are the meeting place for the birthing of God's reality.

He also reminded us that if we aren't thinking about higher things we aren't going to produce higher things. He promoted "elevated thinking." If we keep thinking on and speaking positively about our future, that old climate will eventually break and a shift will take place producing a supercharged atmosphere for breakthrough, miracles, and open doors to discharge and overtake our realities.

So, many of us just need to keep saying the right things and eventually they will show up. Realize though, that in some cases you are breaking a negative field and eventually the right atmosphere will emerge and discharge to you the electrical current of your words. If we have been declaring something and it seems that it's not showing up, it may not be our confession but our atmosphere.

Sometimes we need to change what's in the atmosphere before we throw out our faith. If we throw out faith in a negatively charged field, it will paralyze our words. So begin taking authority over the atmosphere of your money, relationships, and body. Step into mental peak performance by disciplining your thoughts to change the energy of your spiritual umbrella. Speak and decree, "My atmosphere is changing." Begin to declare, "I recharge the atmosphere over my finances, relationships, and life."

Break up that fallow ground, shift the field, and dismantle negative forces. You can expect things to change, as new clouds will begin to emerge and store up the good things you've been saying. Soon, there will be a discharge of opportunity, and great doors are going to open up for you because you are deciding your destiny and empowering your own personal life with the atmosphere you are creating through thoughts and words. This is how you enforce or transmit your spiritual authority as a position of power, influence, and advantage in the earth and in your personal life.

Breaking Contracts

Many times negative energy wants to take over your atmosphere and invade your thoughts with faithless, unbelieving statements and words. You may hear negative things that try to influence what you say about yourself and draw them into your atmosphere.

The truth of the matter is nothing anyone says to you has the power to come to pass unless you agree with it. One of the ways Kingdoms function is by the law of agreement. It simply says: *nothing can take shape in my life unless I've agreed with it in some shape, form or fashion.*

Many of us have made contracts with negative forces because we believed the wrong principles. What we have to do is break those contracts with our words. We have to disagree with what's been said. We have to say something different or else what was said will continue lingering in our future and governing our realities.

I remember when one of our staff members had come down with gall bladder disease, but was healed by applying this same principle. She realized that she had been creating the right atmosphere for what the doctor and others had been saying to by not cutting off their words.

During one of our leadership trainings, I taught on this concept of breaking contracts and changing your atmosphere. She grasped the principles and began to apply them on the way home. One of her confessions was, "I disagree with gall bladder disease and every negative word that has been spoken. I do not agree with you." What was she doing? She was exercising her spiritual power seat.

The results from here were inevitable. Her atmosphere changed and her new words began to take root. Within seven days of her confessing the Word she went to the doctor only to find that there were no signs of the disease anymore. She was completely healed! I want to ask, what about you? What have you been saying for so long about a particular thing that doesn't agree with the language of life? It's time to break the contract, sever the ties with those bad communication waves, and give permission for something new to break forth in your atmosphere.

Take time to examine and acknowledge things that you may have released into your atmosphere that would sabotage your future. Flee from gossip, stop slandering, and commit to subjecting your tongue to words of life, peace, and prosperity. I've learned that when negativity about others is released from our mouths, we disempower ourselves and our language authority.

Be sure to examine your heart, forgive others, and speak blessings over them, not curses. In that way you will continually be speaking life and supercharging your environment with good things. You will build up a tangible release of God's favor and power in your life. You have the power to change your atmosphere. Take authority and begin causing your spiritual climate to shift. Right now you can begin attracting good things to you with life giving words of faith, favor, and increase.

Principles for Empowering Your Life

So, as we covered previously, God's communication and language system is called prayer. More specifically, that language of heaven is the language of life. God only speaks life to all things and to all matters. The reality is, unless we learn to start speaking life to every area of our life, we will limit heaven's ability to influence our atmosphere. Now, before it seems like this book is turning into another read on positive confession, I want to be clear that life is truth and the highest form of reality. With this mind, it is important to view life as a concept of supreme truth and living versus just speaking positively to all matters.

Now, a natural byproduct of speaking God's language is generally positive words, because it delivers positive charges to your atmosphere through sound waves. His language flows from His intention to bless us and prosper us. When you allow God's intention to guide your words, you are effectively operating the language system of heaven. This is the true essence of prayer, allowing God's heart to become the source of our communication.

So, unless you are speaking favor, blessing, and the best possible outcome over every circumstance of your life, your language isn't lining up with the communication system of heaven. I'd like to draw from a familiar scripture verse below:

> *Death and life are in the power of the tongue, and they*
> *who indulge in it shall eat the fruit of it [for death or life]*

> Proverbs 18:21 (AMP)

Again, *life* is the language system of heaven. *Death* is the language system of Babylon. This presents an irrefutable law of language: any time you are speaking, regardless of what you are saying, you can only be speaking one of two languages, life or death. Either *life* is charging your words or *death* is inspiring them. We have to be accountable to this law at all times, because the language we speak depends on the Kingdom that is governing our life. More importantly, heaven's ability to influence our affairs will be limited if our language is being governed by the system outside of God's communication.

From here on out you should begin to focus your thoughts on the power of this present reality: *As I am charging my environment with the sound of heaven, I am empowering my life. I am unleashing my redeemed rights as a Kingdom citizen to control my atmosphere, my position of influence, and my overall potential to produce victorious outcomes.*

Power Concepts from this Chapter

❖ When Adam accepted the idea that he was not made in the likeness and image of God, he opened the door to a new system of thought to govern his life.

❖ God's Kingdom and Satan's kingdom are diametrically opposed. Both rule through concepts of *life* and *death*. You must choose which concept will rule your life.

❖ Before Adam ate from the tree of the knowledge of good and evil, he only knew what God had taught him, which was life (good).

❖ When you speak things, you are charging your atmosphere and attracting what you say into your life.

❖ Make "I am" statements based on the characteristics, qualities, habits, and relationships that you want to attract in your life.

❖ Nothing anyone says to you has the power to come to pass unless you agree with it.

The Blueprint of Praying: The Laws of Clarity

6

For he was looking forward to the city with foundations, whose architect and builder is God.

Hebrews 11:11

The Architect's Plan

Before a single layer of foundation is laid to any building an architect must draw a plan of schematics detailing everything, from the exact size of each room to the distance in between them. This is called "architectural planning." An architectural plan is the design plan and exact description of the architectural elements of a building project, including sketches, drawings, and any other details. In the architectural planning phase, details are the most important part. In fact, the end game of architectural design is to convey enough information that builders are able to recognize a design.

In the same sense, the power of prayer is truly unleashed only when we become clear and detailed about what it is we want. We have to begin seeing ourselves as spiritual architects drafting up schematics to give to our master builder, God. Prayer can be an effective tool only when we decide to become clear accurate sketch artists detailing the design of our greatest wishes and desires. God's plan through this is to help us target and pinpoint what we are really after, not just in prayer but also in life. As Kingdom citizens it is critical that we represent God's government as people of purpose and destiny. We should be clear-minded goal setters in constant pursuit of clearly defined goals.

So, if you want to increase the effectiveness of your praying, then you must challenge yourself to take the time to truly decide and clarify what it is exactly you want to see happen through your request. What is the end result you want to have? What is your main objective? What is important to you this season in your life? These are the questions you have to start asking yourself in order to tap into an unlimited prayer life.

When Jesus told us, "Ask what you desire and it will be given to you," He didn't mean to ask generally. He didn't mean to nonchalantly toss up any kind of prayer to God in hopes that He will answer it. Neither did He mean for us to leave the accuracy of our requests up to God. There are many things God is responsible for when it comes to prayer; however, one thing He isn't responsible for is how clear we indicate what we desire. This part of praying can only be controlled by us.

That's why it is vital that we treat our prayer requests like vivid imageries before we actually pray for them. What I mean is, we have to see it and picture exactly what it is that we want before confess or decree it. Our confession, again, is spiritual law. It functions based on a fixed invariable principle God established and built into creation. And like the detailed schematics of an architectural drawing, our requests have to become the floor plans of our greatest dreams. We have to fix our thoughts and have laser focus in order to build a psychology of confidence and clarity. We have to fix our thoughts to mirror God's Word.

Out of this paradigm of clarity, bold confessions go forth releasing the Word to function in its full and complete power. As we speak the will of God with clarity concerning our deepest desires, our words are like a hammer driving through the backend of a nail. And with each decree and bold request the nail drives deeper into the atmosphere of the universe, releasing those invisible laws of creation to attract blessings.

There may be some seemingly big requests you've asked God for, but you weren't very clear about it. I want to encourage you to go back and meditate until a clear picture of what you desire to see becomes specific and detailed. Imagine you are an architect designing the layout of your greatest dreams. It's up to you to draw the floor plans and measure the rooms. You have to decide how clear you are going to be about what God has promised you. Once you have received the download about what God is saying to you, then you have to become clear about the details. In fact, as you meditate, it's actually the Spirit of God who paints a clear drawing in your imagination for you to call out and ask for.

Be bold today. Be the architect of your life. Meditate until God releases clear pictures of your desires and turn them into bold and faith-filled confessions that will deliver you into your next season and dimension of ultimate blessing.

The Floor Plan of Confession

One type of architectural planning that exists is called *floor plans*. Floor plans include bathrooms, sinks, and rooms. The objective of a floor plan is to be able to scale the features of one specific level of structure. In a building each level has a floor plan because each level has different elements. When we transform our word power into powerful confessions we are laying the floor plans of our desires. With the law of confession we go beyond the surface of prayer into detailed expressions of what we desire to see. Just like each floor needs a floor plan, each dimension of your request needs a new confession. You may be believing God for a new building for your church or company so you ask for it. The next thing God wants to know is, how big of a building? You have to decide and make an accurate confession about it. You've got to decide how big the building is by clarifying within your thoughts how many rooms, the size of those rooms, how they will be used, etc.

Now, you may be wondering at this point, *does this really matter?* I can assure you that specifically praying in detail about what you desire to see is the most effective and efficient way to produce results with prayer. You have to compare God to the builder or contractor. How can a builder successfully construct a building without floor plans? How can he meet your desires without an architectural drawing? In the same token, how can God effectively grant our desires without clarity of what we want? We have to go beyond wanting it, to detailing it. In many cases if the request is that big, it is important to take the time to meditate and listen for God's heart about it. Meditate until the Word becomes clear about your desire and how God wants to use it. Then meditate some more, clarify your thinking, and decide some of the schematics and details.

If it's a new property or facility you want, take time to actually go and visit that facility by bringing it before God, for the Holy Spirit to shape the right picture within your imagination. Then, begin to write. Write what you see, the details and everything. Be clear and acute. This is your floor plan; this is your schematic drawing. Then once you've clarified the details, release your faith and make bold confessions of what you have received. Once you've done this, rest your faith and wait for a response. God may actually say something immediately, like release an idea or instruction or show you the face or name of someone that you need to talk to. Whatever it is, simply follow the next instruction from the Master Builder and He will show you how to turn requests into reality.

When you are making those confessions, don't underestimate the power of spiritual law. Understand that the sound waves from your mouth are activating a force so powerful that you could see breakthrough that same day. The force of confession laid the foundations of the universe. Your confession should flow from what God has already promised you as you clarify your thoughts in order to align them with His. When this happens, nothing will stop your faith-filled requests. No barriers or delay will stand in the way because you've operated spiritual law accurately.

To function in this spiritual law of confession more effectively, picture your request as a building. On each level, make at least one accurate and detailed confession about it. For example, if you want financial increase, believe and receive you that have it. That's the first floor. However, before it comes you need to think about what financial increase looks like to you. That's the second floor. Then decide how much increase exactly you want God to bring to that area. That's the third floor. As you see it with detail and clarity, confess it boldly and with confidence. This type of financial confession would look something like this: *Father, I confess that I have financial increase. I thank you that my salary is being raised, and I command that it increases $300 per month.*

If you are not used to being clear about your prayers, this may seem a little uncomfortable at first. I encourage you though, to keep doing this. Make sure you are taking time to meditate about each "floor" of your confession and raise your expectation of receiving. See, clarifying your prayer is an act of expectation at work. The more you are sure that you have received, the clearer and bolder you will be about what you confess for. Remember, whatever you desire you are to ask for, but only as kings ask, which is with boldness and clarity. The scripture is clear that we will receive because that is how expectation operates. In one occasion we're told to believe that we've received and we will have it. This means receiving is not the physical part. Receiving is the moment of utter psychological and internal persuasion that it's finished. It's in the moment in which we become compelled by an excitement and anticipation of blessing that we verbally declare what we've received.

This is how the law of confession is to be operated. This is where we receive the Word, and the grace of spiritual law begins to attract level by level and floor by floor the design and the plans of our Master Builder's promises. Jeremiah 29:11 reminds us that God knows *His* plans. That word *plans* fits exactly into what we are saying about the science of clarity and the blueprint of praying. God's plans are His architectural drawings and He's waiting to release those to us through consistency in meditation and the power of making bold declaration over our lives. God's plans aren't to harm us. You can pray knowing that God possesses an architectural blueprint that works in our favor.

The "Para"digm Plan

It's so important that we cover critical areas of prayer, such as confession, because it helps us understand the prayer paradigm better. The word *paradigm* literally comes from "two." Prayer has two sides to it: listening and receiving from God, but also exercising boldness and speaking what we desire to see come to pass. Listening of course is the most important part, and as we become more acclimated to hearing first, then receiving and declaring, we will find that prayer is ordered to operate a certain way: by the King's will. As we follow that order we will see greater results when making requests.

Always remember that you are partners with God. You are co-heir with Christ, designing and building your world along with the thoughts, will, and intention of your Governor. Press into God's heart for a clearer perspective and viewpoint of His desires for you. Give your desires to Him and you will find that your initial wants are simply divine trigger points designed to lead you back to God's ultimate purpose and strategy for you.

In Mark 11:12-26, Jesus speaks to a fig tree to never bear fruit again, and only a day later it was withered from its roots. One account of this story indicates that Jesus "answered" unto the tree.

It wasn't that Jesus was answering the tree itself, it's that He was [answering] God by [saying unto] the tree "May no one ever eat fruit from you again." He was responding to God's will, what God showed Him, and His response came out in a bold confession that literally defied the laws of time.

In the same passage, Jesus teaches His disciples that it's possible to command a mountain to throw itself into the sea and it will obey. He didn't say command the mountain to simply move. That's too general. Jesus said if you tell it where to move it will do exactly that. He was saying, *"Somehow it will happen."* This is how the laws of confession are governed, with specificity and clarity. Jesus also reminded the disciples (and us) that receiving is the key. He said, "Do not doubt in your heart." Again, you must build your psychology back into the receiving mechanism God created it to be.

Be sure about what you see, and receive it, leaving no room for doubt. For this is where your power in confession lies: the confident expectation in your heart. The new you that is breaking forth is sure and confident about God's Word. You will have accurate interpretation of God's will and begin speaking things directly into your life far beyond anyone's imagination. Are you willing to take this challenge? Will you begin to think like an architect and design your requests with skill and accuracy? This is where your prayer life will change and those seemingly impossible requests are going to be answered as they begin coming to pass one by one through the power and simplicity of the law of clarity.

Design Barriers

The paradigm of prayer is also powerful because it reminds us that we have to take on a certain mentality when we pray. The prayer paradigm represents not only the two-way street of prayer, but also God's prerequisite of our undivided attention when we pray. God needs our full attention in order to download His thoughts as perfect images that display His will and plan for us.

However, when distractions are heavy, we are unable to see into God's plan and are left with the constant uncertainty of what He wants for us, even after we pray. Have you ever wondered how you can pray for understanding or wisdom to make a decision and you are still left undecided about what to do? It's because your thoughts are too many; you are distracted and your attention is divided.

The purpose of the listening end of prayer is to empower you to receive from God, unhindered and uninterrupted by negative sound waves. That's one of the reasons we must manage our words throughout the day. As I've said, sound is a law that is always at work. If we don't manage our sound with life throughout the day, then our frequency will be tuned to negativity and darkness. Then when we seek to hear from God, bad sound waves will mistune our frequency, keeping us from being able to accurately discern the will of God for our situations. Don't let this be you. Instead, flee from conversations and words that breed death. Don't let the toxic sound waves of fear invade your atmosphere.

Once you've mastered the power of staying on the frequency of life at all times, you will see your divine communication levels rise. The common distractions that were bombarding your thoughts during prayer will fade away. You will have clarity and focus on what God is thinking as He fills your imagination and thoughts with ideas and plans flowing directly from His heart. What I am saying to you is, the prayer paradigm cannot be accurately operated unless you clear the airwaves. You have to detox from negativity and learn to create a psychological atmosphere of peace at all times. That's why Matthew 6:28 reminds us that people with worry and distractions in their heart babble in prayer.

You see, worry causes distractions and those distractions inhibit your ability to think clearly. You can't perceive what God is thinking when you are distracted about paying bills, or the negativity that went on that day. Remember, prayer is a paradigm, and it will not be effective unless both sides are operated in order and in alignment with God's peace. Without that peace, distractions take over, causing our prayers to become worrisome and wordy, because we're unable to detect a sure and definite response from God's heart that there is a plan working on our behalf. No matter what you are facing at this point in your life, you must refuse to let the negative voices in life overpower God's voice in you.

You need to rest your thoughts and detox from the negativity that is surrounding you so that you can receive precise downloads concerning the architectural design for your life. Imagine that your prayers are like a blueprint developing in a dark room and the floor plans to your next breakthrough. You need the peace and silence of a clear mind to make accurate distinctions about what you want and where you want to go next in your life. Once you've regained peace and stilled your thoughts from every distraction, prepare to receive clear instruction from your Chief Designer that will change your life.

8 Powerful Ways to Disable Distractions

1. Set the trajectory of your day by choosing your thoughts.
2. Meditate on the Word often to produce enriched thoughts.
3. Limit the time you spend with people who are negative.
4. Refrain from discussions that are not fruitful.
5. Avoid conversations that concentrate on negativity.
6. Seclude yourself various times daily to speak good things.
7. Use the Word to challenge negative and fearful thoughts.
8. Take a deep breath before you pray and detox your mind.

The Architect, The Builder

In my own personal life I've witnessed the power of applying the laws of clarity that I have shared with you in this chapter. I started to apply the spiritual side of prayer, versus the physical labor part. I've learned that when I desire to see a result in something, that desire isn't inspired by me; it's actually flowing from God's life in me, His Spirit, charging my thoughts with His plans.

If I am careful to meditate on the desire within my heart, it never fails that I begin to receive simultaneous downloads from Heaven. Many times I don't have to speak a word; just simply acknowledging God with my thoughts is powerful enough to invoke a clear Word from Him. As I seek God's will and clarify my desires, often times I have to begin writing as He reveals clarifying thought after clarifying thought of the plans He has for me.

This is the original design of prayer. This is the spiritual consequence of entering into the Kingdom of God through Jesus and becoming heirs of His promise. The communication system that Adam lost in the garden, we have recovered through Christ. We have inherited a righteous communion that enables us to know exactly what God is thinking about us at anytime. We simply have to learn the paradigm power of prayer to tap in. There is an incredible and divine plan waiting to unfold in every area of your life.

So, your thoughts have the power to invoke the laws of prayer. This is why the scripture says, "As a man thinks in his heart so is he." God wasn't simply saying that we become whatever we think. Actually, we think a lot of things that thankfully, by God's grace, we don't actually become. This scripture not only indicates the prayer power of our thoughts but also the power of consistent thinking. You see, as we think we become, or in other words, *What we think right now is what and who we are right now.* So as we think, we take on the characteristics and nature of the government our thoughts reflect.

This scripture gives incredible insight on how we can be in God's government but still miss His Blessing. We actually have all we need through the government of heaven inside of us. However, what we think or choose to believe, determines in that moment the state or kingdom we are representing. So, as we think on provision being met we are functioning in God's government. But, as we think opposite to that and worry about how needs will be met, we take on characteristics of Babylonian government. So then, by choosing to align with this protocol of praying, we choose to take on both sides of prayer, balancing the power of confession with the vital component of listening. As I said, this principle changed my life. At one point in my life, it seemed as though nothing was happening for me. I was frustrated about the results I was getting financially, emotionally, and relationally. One day, while making confessions, it simply dawned on me that I had been frustrated because all this time I was leaving out the listening part of prayer.

From there I began to apply listening, and then I begin learning to clarify my thoughts. I began realizing different things I had asked for that got answered, but because I was so general I didn't recognize the answer when it showed up. I realized how badly my lack of clarity was affecting my voice. By voice I mean my authority. I was short-changing myself and cutting off my inheritance as a citizen in the Kingdom by not applying these clearly outlined principles in the Word. It tells us to ask "what" we desire. They key is "what?" What is it exactly that you want to see happen. I mean, what specifically do you see? Make your thoughts clear. It's okay to take time to clarify things; you don't have to pray immediately for something just because it came to mind. Sometimes God will spend days clarifying His heart to us. Take this time to write down what you specifically want.

The floor plans to an exciting future are one confession away. Your best days are ahead of you waiting to become your present reality. I believe that today, your paradigm is conforming to the original plan of the Creator. You are about to lay the schematic drawings of your desires and unleash them into the atmosphere to manifest. This is not about just trying to get something from God.

However, this is one side of your inheritance and your divine right to be blessed. You must gain a bold attitude that you have the right to take advantage of every benefit, opportunity, and privilege the Kingdom affords you.

We cannot afford to leave out this clarity principle when seeking real effective results with praying. I become concerned when I hear people say that God doesn't speak to us that clearly or that actually hearing detail from God is "crazy." You see, Noah could not have built the arc if it wasn't for his ability to hear clear, sound and acute instruction. When God told Moses how to build His temple, just like with Noah, He gave clear instruction and measurements on how to build it. Everything was specifically given through detailed instruction, from the person who was supposed to make the priests' garment to how much gold was to be used on the offering table. God wears two hats when it comes to our life's blueprint. Hebrews 11:10 says He is 1) architect and 2) the master builder. Those clarifying thoughts we have been discussing flow from God's blueprint. He is the one who gives us clear images of what to ask for and declare. On the other end, He is the builder, taking what we have spoken and, with detail, bringing our confessions to pass.

I realized, that our ability to clarify what we want isn't necessarily about how much we can see, but more so, it's about how well we can see into God's unlimited imagination concerning His plan for us. Remember that the purpose of the architectural plan is so that the builder can recognize a design. The laws of clarity dictate; without clarity God does not recognize our prayers. By aligning and integrating our prayers with the conceptual principle of design, we'll most certainly enable blessings to show up exactly where needed.

Power Concepts from this Chapter

- ❖ Prayer can be an effective tool only when we decide to become clear, accurate sketch artists detailing the design of our greatest wishes and desires.
- ❖ As we speak the will of God with clarity concerning our deepest desires, our words are like a hammer driving through the backend of a nail.
- ❖ Your confession should flow from what God has already promised you as you clarify your thoughts in order to align them with His.
- ❖ Prayer has two sides to it: listening and receiving from God, but also exercising boldness and speaking what we desire to see come to pass.
- ❖ Without peace, distractions take over causing our prayers to become worrisome and wordy, because we're unable to detect a sure and definite response from God's heart that there is a plan working on our behalf.
- ❖ God wears two hats when it comes to our life's blueprint. He is 1) architect and 2) the master builder.

The Power of the Tongue: The Birth Canal of the Supernatural

7

He chose to give us birth through the word of truth that we might be a kind of first fruits of all he created.

James 1:18

The System of Life and Death

The very panoply of creation is founded on the principle of sound. In Genesis 1 we witness the account of the creation of all existence. There is nothing that was created that didn't originate with sound. The Word of God literally streamlined God's sound into creation and began to birth out the vision of God's heart. Everything seen and unseen finds its origination in the power of sound.

That is the power of God's sound or His Word. He transmitted His light waves into the earth producing the Garden of Eden for man to live in. It was His Kingdom taking physical shape in the earth realm through the power of spoken sound. In John 1, the writer tells us that in the beginning was the Word and that all things have been made through this Word. Well, here the Word is referring to the system of life; it's the sound of God's heart. However, in Genesis 1 the writer explains that in the beginning God created the heavens and Earth and He began to speak earth into existence. This is because Genesis 1 highlights the "spoken word" and John 1 targets the *logos* Word or the "thought Word."

What God was thinking on in John 1, He was speaking out of His mouth in Genesis 1. God was transmitting the sound waves of His heart concerning His blessed Kingdom for mankind to experience with all of its richness and abundance.

You see, the Kingdom of Life (light) is simply transmitted through the sound of God's Word. The kingdom of death (darkness) is translated by the sound waves of fear and negativity. When someone speaks life they are literally translating the authority of heaven's Kingdom into the affairs of earth. When they speak death or unfavorably about things they empower the same kingdom of that sound, death, to produce and manifest in their own reality.

Whether we realize this or not, without sound waves being channeled through our mouths neither kingdom can be permitted to function in the earth realm because the earth is ruled by the human kingdom. God is a spirit; that's why He functions by sound. A spirit is literally the highest sound of supreme energy. That energy is its thoughts. That's why in the beginning (John 1) God was thinking (logos, thought). He only had an idea because that is what a spirit is, a conscious being that operates in the highest level of consciousness.

So God, the supreme conscious being, spoke His supreme sound and created the heavens and earth. So the human kingdom rules planet earth and the spirit kingdom rules the unseen terrain. When God, who is spirit, wants to influence earth, He needs foreign aid from individuals in the earth realm because it is ruled by the kingdom of humans. God established this law of creation Himself in Genesis 1: 28 when He said:

Be fruitful and increase in number; fill the earth and subdue it. Rule over the fish in the sea and the birds in the sky and over every living creature that moves on the ground.

Here God made it clear that mankind is to be the supreme kingdom ruling in planet earth, not spirits. Though man is a spirit first, he was created with a flesh and soul, giving him rights as a new hybrid species called "human." So, in order to tangibly express any kingdom of sound in the earth, whether it is life or death, it must be channeled through the mouth of a human being.

This is so important to understand because our awareness of these principles will give greater understanding as to what really perpetuates the things showing up in our lives. Did you know that your enemy isn't after your money, your family, or any of your possessions? He is after your tongue.

The reality is that the spiritual dynamics that surround the authentic operation of spiritual jurisdictions in your life are simply subsistent as waging bids for your tongue. The major systems that control this world are kingdoms ruled by spirits. Therefore, you must be careful of what words you choose. As a human being, you possess the legal authority through your tongue to legalize foreign policies and the influence of spiritual governments concerning life or death into the kingdom of planet earth.

Premium Real Estate

The concept of life and death expresses the process of conceiving an idea rather than producing one. See, if you're going to say anything, whether positive or negative, it is going to flow from the womb of your heart. In other words, our mind is the conception place for kingdom principles or ideas to cultivate and our mouth is where we give birth to that system in our tangible life.

Those ideas are shaped by our perception, which is governed by the sound we choose to take in. When a particular sound is prevalent in our life it will naturally shape a perception within us. Then that perception will become the channel through which ideas pass and make themselves at home within our minds.

The more comfortable the space is for unfavorable ideas to live in us, the more likely we are to give birth to sounds that don't generate positive outcomes. However, if we are willing to change the sound we take in we can easily change the type of houseguest we have staying within the confines of our spiritual home.

Sound has the ability to totally change us from the inside out, perception-by-perception and thought-by-thought. An edifice is being built with every sound we choose to entertain and influence our minds. If God's Kingdom is going to show up tangibly in our lives, it will be because He's built a comfortable living space in the real estate of our minds. You see, your heart is spiritual real estate and your perceptions build homes or living structures that rent out space to ideas and thoughts. Those ideas are like houseguests. It can easily tell who we have living with us by the sound we continue to make. When Jesus comes into our hearts it isn't to lease or rent space, it's to claim full possession of our internal paradigm so that He can be in control of what shapes our perceptions.

So the very premeditation of Jesus's heart when He preached, *"The Kingdom of heaven is at hand,"* was completely inspired by God's motive to translate His government to us through sound perceptions governed by the principles of His heart. You see the word *hand* in Hebrew actually represents the *heart*. It is a reference point that indicates what *"we grasp with our heart."*

Like many of Jesus' sayings, the statement *"the Kingdom is at hand"* is a pictorial expression of the human's capability to literally grasp and take back authority with God's Kingdom through His mind. So, the intangible government of heaven can become realer than we can imagine if we are willing to turn over the leasing space of our internal paradigm structures to God's Word and His sound.

The Eviction Notice

The power of spiritual reality should not be taken lightly. It gives the understanding of what God's Kingdom comes to do in our hearts. As I said before, the mind is like spiritual real estate and our thoughts become the tenants we are leasing space too. As we come further to the reality of impact that sound has in our life, we can easily tell what tenants need to go and which ones can stay.

In order to have a real impact with your prayer life, you must get rid of ideas that have been shaped by perceptions that didn't come from God. This is necessary because those tenants are influencing your words, which produces the outward sound that determines which government rules your life.

In Matthew 12:43-45, Jesus reminds us that when thoughts (or spirits) are cast out they come back to see if there is a comfortable place for them to live. You see, on the outside we may only see flesh and a body, but internally we are a house. We are foreign terrain that God wants to conform into a province of heavenly influence through our conscious state of being.

However, we have to make room for His Kingdom to build the right internal structures that house God's power and authority in our lives. In order do that we have to serve those negative, fear-based thoughts an eviction notice. You should begin exposing those negative thoughts and declaring these words over yourself: *It's time for every thought uninspired by God's favor to go. From this point on I will only entertain ideas and beliefs empowered by the sound of life.*

A recent study on the cognitive effects of substance abuse relapse showed that the mental state of individuals who return to destructive habits shape patterns in their brains that create behaviors consistent with them. Another study showed that relapse of any kind is only preventable by the changing of previous thought patterns created. Similarly if we aren't willing to serve an eviction notice on thoughts and ideas that do not endorse God's frequency of life within us then we will continually be subject to the same (wave) patterns of sound that continue transmit the wrong signal into our life. As a result, we will continue in cycles of unanswered prayer and unfavorable outcomes because we are relapsing back into the controlled substance of negative thoughts and negative sounds.

You have the power to change what patterns you produce with your words by changing the tenants of your thoughts. Press the delete button on every idea and belief system that is contrary to God's Word and riots against His plan of favor to bring you into the lifestyle of constant communication and answered prayer.

Within your heart you possess premium real estate and the ability to fully grasp the authority of God's Kingdom by allowing His sound to shape your internal perceptions. By doing this you are unleashing your ability to produce life giving patterns and supercharged frequencies of favor with the power of your tongue.

Your successful Kingdom communication will simply be a natural by-product of the joint partnership you've created with God by making room in your heart for His government to acquire the internal leasing space and property of your mind.

Internalizing Kingdom Perception

When you yield your paradigm to the concept and system of life, you have inwardly positioned yourself to become navigated by the internal compass of God's heart. Your spiritual house can now be designed according to God's plan concerning all matters of your life. As you tune your heart to the sound of your new born again nature, inward perceptions become divine jurisdictions of heaven's internal authority literally changing the panoply of your life from the inside out.

Now you will be able to perceive correctly God's will and plan for you as you navigate the internal compass of His life within. You are literally unleashing God's invisible blueprint. As your internal paradigms align with His pathways you are changing and redefining your spiritual trajectories while coming into agreement with a system, plan and reality designed to elevate you to levels of unlimited living.

The culmination of this unique plan finds its substance and takes emergence through the birth canal of our words. Our tongue can be our best friend or our worst enemy. It all depends on what kingdom we internalize the most.

You know, God is a navigation expert. He can show us how to win in everything. The more we concentrate on the new life that has been translated to us by the Kingdom of Light, the more we'll be able to speak God's language accurately and consistently. It is important to confess and declare the Word daily, but in constituency with an intentional effort to remain consciously aware of the sound of heaven operating within us as complete beings reflecting God's image.

The more we look at our new nature within the more this power of our limited flesh nature loses its authority over us. We have to understand that we are spirits designed in God's likeness. Everything the Bible says we received is within our new redeemed spirit. We literally are new beings, complete and whole.

You have to see yourself this way if you are going to successfully operate the laws of prayer. Remember, God's language is prayer and its system functions by the law of sound. That sound is continually active when we are petitioning to God and when we are not. Staying focused on the Kingdom within will allow us to see ourselves for who we really are outside of our flesh. The more we actualize this new nature within us we are begin transformed into the God-life that's been stored away in our spirit. When this happens nothing will be able to contain us.

The Signature Sound of Words

Although this may contradict what the five senses are dictating to us daily, we have received total redemption and recovery back into the provision policy and plan of Eden. Through our tongues we literally possess the power to determine the reinitiating of Eden's government in the earth. This time it has to be us who speaks the Blessing of life. The will of Adam, which represents the will of man, interrupted God's original plan. Now that we have been restored, it's up to us to exchange that will with God's policy of favor once again. Our tongues are the signature pens that contract words to go forth and produce a tangible substance.

When Adam made that negative confession of himself, he contracted another government to produce the offspring of his words. He had internalized a different government, which produced the state of his communication. Jesus came and restored that communication with the signature pen of His blood and the word of His testimony. That same truth is how we overcome the political power of darkness in this life. A good reference to this is found in Revelation 12:10-11:

> *Now have come the salvation and the power and the kingdom of our God, and the authority of his Messiah…. They triumphed over him by the blood of the Lamb and by the word of their testimony.*

Notice that the authority of the Kingdom is manifested through words. Although we have overcome every obstacle and challenge, we have to understand that our tongues are what contract the rights of this inheritance to take form in our tangible life. Furthermore, the word *testimony* actually means *covenant* in Greek. It literally says here that our words inspired by the triumph of the blood literally form a covenant or contract to manifest that overcomer's lifestyle.

Now look at what it says concerning the signature power of our tongues in this scripture verse:

My tongue is the pen of a skillful writer.

Psalm 45:1

Again the tongue has contract power through the signature of our sound. And when we have internalized the authority of Jesus' blood we cause our tongues to be cleansed by His truth. That truth is the birthing place of all answered prayer. So, in this way our tongues become the pen of a ready writer, contracting words of life, prosperity and healing through the triumphant power of Jesus' blood.

Whenever God spoke a promise in His Word it was His signature. That is why the scriptures say in Hebrews 10:15, *"This covenant will I make with them…I will write my words on their hearts and I will write them in their minds."* God wants us to internalize His Word written in our new, born again spirit until the signature of His words forms a covenant in our minds. Then we will speak those same things with consistency creating favorable contracts for our future.

Regardless of how things may look you can have faith in the face of adversity if you'll commit to speaking the right things. Even when it seems like you're losing everything you'll still have the confidence to declare: *My future is favorable based on the King's word I have spoken out of my heart. God has made a contract to bless me according to His penmanship on my heart.*

Whether you've realized it or not you are the author of your life. With every word you release you are writing your destiny. The possibilities are endless when you realize you literally get to write your own story. Your tongue is the pen of a ready and skillful writer. When you decide to agree with the words God is already saying about you, you are internalizing His sound and choosing to write your history with contracts of life through the signature power of the tongue.

Unleash Your Signature Life

Think for a moment, that with your tongue you are writing your history before it happens. You never have to agree with the outcomes that negative forces of life are trying to dictate to you. You can always change your story, you can always write a different ending. In fact, that ending is found in Jeremiah 29:11:

> *For I know the thoughts and plans that I have for you,*
> *says the Lord, thoughts and plans for welfare and peace*
> *and not for evil, to give you hope in your final outcome.*

Your final outcome is already decided. Our authority lies in our ability to leverage heaven's predesigned outcome into prayer power. Our confidence in God's plan to prosper us and not to harm us should release the sound of bold and life-charged petitions enforcing God's covenant of life into our affairs. Those petitions will flow from the signature of God's Word in our heart.

When we are producing our signature sound of prayer we can be sure that a signature life is no longer out of reach. By your signature life, I am referring to Jeremiah 29:11, the final outcome that God has decided concerning His plan of prosperity that will govern your life. You have a life that's tailor-made for you, trademarked by the imprint of your words. God has reserved a life of unique blessings, favorable conditions, and personal experiences that will harmonically work together to produce His signet prosperous plan for you. That plan is written, and in that plan you win and win every time. That's your signature life. Though many people don't realize it, accurate prayer is designed to bring you into your authentic life.

That's a life that can only be forged by the signature of your sound and written by the penmanship of your tongue. When the laws of prayer are understood and operated properly, individuals will tap into a divine plan of diplomacy that is far greater than we could ever imagine. As prayer is the communication system of heaven, and the mouth is birthing place of that communication, God's Kingdom purpose revolves around strategically using the force of prayer to unleash His unlimited plan of winning favor, victorious outcomes, and trademark living.

The sound you are projecting through the internalization of life's language is enlarging your opportunity to thrive as you come into greater awareness and manifestation of your citizenship in the Kingdom of God. Prayer is about much more than getting our petitions heard. It's about changing systems and changing languages that will coach patterns of internal influences that will point us into the direction of our new born again nature, which as our citizenship in heaven.

Your signature life is the outward expression of the internal position you have accessed as a legal resident of God's country. I want to encourage you to continue to increase your thought capacity concerning prayer as a language system designed to bring you into the complete benefits package of your redeemed rights as heirs to the Kingdom of heaven. As you do, your words will follow God's divine inscriptions within your heart. You'll be praying from the elevated position of your government seat shaped by the internal consciousness of Christ's kingship within.

That kingship is based on the contract of God's supernatural life inside you. Draw from its substance by continuing to focus on what's inside you rather than what's around you. As you do, you'll continue to empower yourself with signature sounds that will authenticate the contract of your God-life within. That life is governed by a winning plan designed to release your signature life through the contractual power of your tongue.

A Matter of Life and Death

Prayer is an instrument of divine influence designed to bring you into the totality of your victorious life. It's designed to release divine intellect concerning God's winning strategy to prosper you through His Kingdom plan of deployment. Remember that you are an ambassador of heaven and your quality of life is dependent upon your ability to access and enforce the King's plan in your life.

When we are praying according to the Kingdom order, we are releasing that divine intellect into active perpetuation that can give us a position of advantage in any area of life. However, that position of advantage can quickly change into a defeated position if our tongues aren't trained in God's Word.

Here is an essential truth that all Christians need to be aware of if they expect to have effective prayer lives: Your tongue can lose the battle. Remember there is a waging bid for your tongue, but not just when you're making requests to God. If you examine it closely you realize there is always a sound trying to influence what you're saying regularly. You have to remember that prayer is the law of language and sound. All creation exists within those laws. I cannot express to you how important it is that we understand this principle.

What you're saying in one area of your life is distinctly tied to what you're saying about something else. All the time the laws of sound that govern creation are taking into account the energy waves you are releasing through words.

If you make a powerful petition to God concerning your finances but turn around and speak unfavorably about someone else, you are jeopardizing the power and legitimacy of your words. By avoiding these pitfalls of the tongue we are better positioned for God's overall plan through Kingdom communication to the major source of language producing a continuous harvest of His victorious plan.

The same way God birthed us into existence through the word of truth, is the same way we birth His plan into our lives through the power of the tongue. So, you see, in terms of what you're saying, every situation truly is a matter of life and death. You choose today Eden or Babylon, Blessing or curse, favor or defeat.

The plan for you to win is never too far out of reach. You're always one favorable word away from a victorious outcome. Maybe it's time to serve some eviction notices to some tenants who haven't been paying rent; those are thoughts and ideas that aren't bearing fruit in your life. It's time to lease some new space for a new mindset.

It's time to write a new story and change plans. You have been translated into a new Kingdom and a new you is about to break forth. For your prayers are empowered to release divine influence through the skillful writer of your tongue.

Power Concepts from this Chapter

❖ The Word of God literally streamlined God's sound into creation and began to birth out the vision of God's heart.

❖ Everything seen and unseen finds its origination in the power of sound.

❖ Your heart is spiritual real estate, and your perceptions build homes or living structures that rent out space to ideas and thoughts.

❖ When we realize the impact that sound has in our life we can easily tell which tenants need to go and which ones can stay.

❖ Our tongues are the signature pens that contract words to go forth and produce tangible substance.

❖ Living in the Kingdom of God does not mean that you will never face any tough circumstances in your life. It means that you can tap into God's perspective of your situation in order to produce a positive outcome.

❖ Your signature life is the outward expression of your internal position.

Prayer Evolution: The Adamnomics of Praying

8

Ask of Me, and I will give You the nations as Your inheritance, and the uttermost parts of the earth as Your possession.

Psalm 2:8 (AMP)

Seasoned Maturity

At this point you're probably realizing that your paradigm of prayer is enlarging itself much greater than what it previously was. That's because you've now taken prayer outside the box of one-time happenings and you are starting to view it as a cultural power tool of divine influence. The more you see prayer as the language system of life, the simpler yet more powerful it becomes in your life.

The major mark of seasoned maturity is one's ability to control their tongue. Now although the Bible says no man can tame the tongue it's important to interject this empowering point: with God all things are possible. When you decide that the value of your words holds your destiny within them you began to alter your mindset and make conscious decisions to become a steward of your mouth.

You begin evolving, not just in how you pray but how you manage your words all together. Now that prayer has become a joint venture between you and God versus a self-effort, His Kingdom system of communication can transform your world from the inside out.

God never intended for prayer to function from the basis of one-time happenings. It was always His plan that our prayer life would transform our entire world. As we gain a more subjective perspective of the Kingdom within us and our power position in that government, the subjective paradigm evolves into an outward perception of life. That perception is triggered by the truth of God's sound continually ringing in our heart to empower us without limits.

When God released His sound into us He invested His plan and overall purpose to see us thrive at all levels. His system of Blessing is marked with His favor, His sign of approval, guaranteeing His promise. The power to unlock those promises is hidden in His Word. The seasoned heart of the believer learns to expect based on this promise. A sure guarantee in God's Word is the point of rest for every true Kingdom citizen.

Prayer is not about what we can accomplish. It's about God strategically using our words as channels of power to release His Kingdom into the earth. The power to produce and manifest our greatest desires is a natural function of Kingdom powered praying. However, we have to graduate and gravitate toward the understanding, that children who mature are the ones who receive their inheritance. James 3:2 (AMP) reminds us of the benefits of seasoned maturity concerning the tongue:

> *And if anyone does not offend in speech [never says the wrong things], he is a fully developed character and a perfect man, able to control his whole body and to curb his entire nature.*

When we determine to move beyond our feelings and emotions into the mature nature of our born again spirit within us we will unlock a hidden power that can propel us into our destiny. One of the ways that power shows up is by supernaturally charging our spirit and our minds with the force of God-inspired thoughts and words. We will be able to determine what conversations we should avoid, negative statements to refrain from, and most of all how to petition effectively. This will have a lasting impact on our prayer power and we will see constant success with praying. Making faith-filled requests and powerful declarations that produce real results will become a tangible experience.

You see the basis for all biblical prosperity is seasoned maturity in the Word of God. Psalm 1:1-3, reminds us that when we meditate on God's sound (word) a seasoned ripening of knowledge is produced. That knowledge then transforms into a powerful plan to prosper you and whatever you put your hands to, and you'll experience great success. Believe it or not, this is supposed to be the daily experience of Christians.

We have the authority to produce God's prosperous will as an advancing mechanism in this earth. When we love His words more than we love our own, they become ours and trigger a spiritual metamorphosis as we become transformed by the renewing of our mind. Spiritual maturity is the end result of the Kingdom process of transformation, meaning you are shedding your old nature and crossing the threshold of permanent change as you embrace the new powerful you.

Allow God's words to infuse yours and produce harmonious agreement with His sound. You'll be releasing your true nature of unlimited power through the divine operation of Kingdom-powered praying. Remember that your seasoned maturity is the mark of real transformation and conformation into the image and likeness of your God-life within. Through this evolving power of prayer you are about to release your season of unstoppable success!

The Power Position of Prayer

Now the unstoppable you is ready to be unleashed. Powered by boldness, accurate prayer language, and spirit-filled words you are renewing your perspective to the benefits package and unwavering rights of your power seat. It is without a doubt that you have truly been raised and seated with Christ (Ephesians 2:6) and as a royal heir you have the responsibility to leverage that chair as a power position of influence on heaven's behalf in the earth.

Real spirit-filled praying is conscious of the God-life within. It's speaking words based on the nature and the reality of your power seat. When you pray from this perspective you gain the paradigm of an influencer leveraging the authority of a winning position to power your prayers into confident and bold petitions that release manifestations of already completed works. See, when you are spirit conscious as you pray, nothing will continue to seem impossible.

Because you are viewing your circumstance through the perspective of the King, who sees all things as finished, His sound is constantly witnessing to your spirit that God is able to bring it to pass. Nothing is too big to ask for and you don't ever have to be intimidated by how big the need is. You see, praying from your power seat empowers you to view seemingly big challenges for what they are by holding those circumstances up against the complete authority of God's hand.

I promise you that in the presence of such truth, everything must bow; even deceptions and mental barriers keeping you from seeing what you already possess as dearly loved children seated in a position of favor and power in God's Kingdom.

It's important to remember that as we leverage the laws of listening we can effectively use every concept and prayer strategy to build consistent barrier-breaking communication with God. Listening helps us to evolve as prayer champions who can see their confidence growing as we concentrate more and more on the perfect picture of our new life within. As that confidence increases, the spiritual principle of prayer evolution demands that one's state of proposal be consistent with his overall state of self-evolution. The more we know about what we possess we should move from a state of need to a position of abundance.

That abundance happens in the mind and is inspired by the confidence one is gradually developing into as a mature thinker. This can take time; however, I want you to see that asking, seeking, and knocking cumulatively represent the powerful order of prayer evolution.

3 Dimensions of Prayer Evolution

Asking:

Represents a basic-level state of internal awareness of our ability to communicate with God. In this phase of prayer evolution we are in the fertility stages of answered prayer.

Here we are able to see some results with prayer, and in many cases little to none. This doesn't mean asking is bad; however, from this standpoint in asking one sees himself or herself as a subject rather than a son. I encourage anyone at this phase to ask away whatever you want from God until your heart is content. However, when it's time to develop into the next stage, answer the call to believe God in a greater dimension!

Seeking:

Seeking is a maturing state of faith and learning how to apply God's Word to get results. Here we are still grasping the understanding of asking and placing a demand for what we have.

In this stage of praying, results are becoming more consistent and we are still being groomed for greater authority in prayer. We have learned to seek God's will to get better results with prayer.

Here the partnership paradigm emerges. Praying from this paradigm is learning how to ask more confidently and boldly by stating demands by faith. Here we also leverage a spiritual perception to perceive a harvest and step out on faith to possess it.

Knocking:

Represents a final evolutionary state of pure confidence in which we no longer see ourselves asking for God to bless us, but we grab ahold of the self-awareness of the Blessing and that life is in our tongue.

Here we know what we possess, how to access it, and how to apply it. From this evolutionary phase we come into greater alignment with heaven's nature in us and begin to pray from the unlimited paradigm position of our power seat in the Kingdom of God. In this phase of praying, confessions and royal decrees are made and boldly stated as God's will for our life with unlimited expectation.

There is no begging here, only a sure confidence that God backs up what we say as we pray with a trained will constantly seeking and submitting to God's intent through our words. A knocking paradigm is excuse-free living. You can leverage this mentality concerning prayer to reclaim man's identity as master communicators with heaven and earth.

When you combine all three phases of prayer evolution you witness a growing stage in each level that brings us closer to our original ruling power with prayer and communication.

Jesus was clear that who asks receives an answer, who seeks will find, and who knocks the door is open. All three stages are significant to answered prayer; however, the final phase of knocking is where there is a clear understanding of how to leverage the law of prayer to open spiritual doors and manifest heavenly activity.

Every believer must evolve to a "knocking" state in which we beg no more and do not doubt our inheritance; instead we mature into a state of high impact praying making confident decrees and bold requests for God to do big things on our behalf in planet earth.

Now, I want to also bring another point into this picture of prayer evolution. Each phase represents a paradigm shift in which we all receive responses from God, but they are dependent on our approach. Let me explain what I mean. You see, Jesus says whoever "asks" will receive an answer. This is a good thing. Now, He also confirms that if you "seek" you will find what you're looking for. This is also good. Now watch, He goes further to say, "But if you have the faith to believe you have received and that you have found, then just go ahead and "knock" and the door will be opened" [Author paraphrase].

You see in all stages Jesus is proposing that our response from God is a direct proponent to our confidence level. In other words your confidence creates the net for receiving your harvest. Our confidence level is how we receive from God through the system of prayer. So, Jesus is saying if you are at an asking level then ask. If you are at a seeking state then seek.

However, if you are confident enough, simply believe you have access then apply force (knock) on the Kingdom law of prayer and you will see results (the door will be opened). It is my personal belief that all stages produce results, but the intent of God is that we evolve through each stage, building confidence in the previous one. We should all be continually maturing into a new level once we have used the benefits of our faith on the previous level.

If you have been asking and receiving for some time, but now it seems you are no longer receiving, it may be time to raise your confidence and move to a seeking state. Believe God for bigger things and enlarge your prayer requests. The same goes if you have been a seeker, your paradigm may need to change to a bolder stance of making sound declarations as you partner with God through your confidence.

This unique perspective on the cumulative power of prayer will build a greater value in your mind for all stages of prayer, and it will also challenge and empower you to raise your faith and believe God for more.

I can personally tell you that in my own life, I saw some amazing results with asking God in my beginning stages of faith. I would ask for everything from material possessions to spiritual abundance and God was faithful to my every request. But something interesting began to happen after a while.

It was as though God was no longer answering my requests. I would ask for the simplest need to be met and still no answer from God. "What is going on?" I began to wonder to myself.

One day, God spoke to me and said, "You have been asking long enough, but I will no longer answer your prayer on this level; you must begin to seek me with more confidence and speak and declare my word."

This changed my life. I realized that God is our father and wants us to grow in every phase of life. He wants our communication with Him to be on the same level He intended, believing with boldness and taking action on His promises. We cannot afford to continue to timidly approach God in prayer as though we have just started out.

I know many Christians believe that if we will take this weak, helpless state of prayer, crying to God for help, He will see us as humble and always answer. This is not so.

God wants us to be bold and to rise to new levels of asking by training our heart to seek His will. Once we become accustomed to a state of partnering with God's will we can boldly declare our desires knowing that we have been validated by the testimony of

His heart. We can be unwavering in the face of spiritual accusations that our prayers will not be heard because we have decreed from the internal position of dominion as joint-heirs and co-creators with God through prayer.

The Adamnomics of Praying

Man's original function as divine beings was always to communicate on the highest levels of consciousness, which is God's Word. God by nature is the highest conscious being that exists; that's what makes Him God: His high level and state of consciousness.

That's His Word or *"logos"* (Greek), which means thought or reason. When we view the Word from this perception we understand this supreme language of heaven only flows from a supreme thought pattern and paradigm. God is the master craftsman of ideas and master of communication and language.

When God created man in His image, He produced another living being able to think like Him and make His sound as well. So you see, God wanted to communicate with other beings on His level of supreme consciousness and state of existence.

This means man's original function was a supreme state of thought and consciousness. In other words, we were created to be supreme thinkers ruling our world with powerful communication through a righteous sound powered by God's imagination.

Our mandate is still the same, and God restored our ability to communicate freely on frequencies the flesh cannot understand. This is what it means to be redeemed into the Kingdom of God again: through the function of prayer you get to reconnect to your original state of communication mastery through your God-life within.

When we speak, every word should be governed by a supreme state of thought. I know this sounds easier than it is to accomplish; however, stick with the behavior pattern of coaching positive life-giving thoughts to empower your mind with. By doing so, you are waking up the sleeping giant within. You are reclaiming access to your power seat.

When man learns to enter into that final stage of boldness and declaration of faith we actually tap into God's original plan for us as unlimited beings able to communicate with Him on His level.

Decreeing is a God-level conscious style of praying and communicating. It's taking back the Kingdom form of prayer by combining asking and seeking together to create an evolutionary stage called knocking. Again this is applied force to the Kingdom law (of prayer).

The Earthly Inheritance Through Communication

Now, the term "Adamnomics" is a personally coined term I use to simply explain the original function of something as it pertains to the original life of Adam and how we should posses it now as redeemed Kingdom citizens through the redemption plan of Jesus Christ.

With that said, I want to explain the function of prayer as a system of release and the overall access point of our Blessing inheritance:

> *He said to me, "You are my son; today I have become your father. Ask me and I will make the nations your inheritance the ends of the earth your possession.*

Psalm 2:8

Notice that God tells us to "ask Him" concerning our inheritance of planet earth. That's right, God's original plan was to give planet earth to us as our inheritance of Blessing and sonship. This doesn't mean we didn't have to possess the earth with the Kingdom first. However, through our seizing of the earth through God's principles it's His intention to share His Kingdom with us by giving us full reign in the earth realm.

I want to be clear that God created earth for the human kingdom to rule. It's important for us to understand this because our right of sonship is key to unlocking real material inheritance in the earth.

Earth was designed to be subjective us. God created it with the same sound of His Word that created you and I. He then placed us over the earth giving us dominion over every Kingdom and making us stewards of His sound. This made us supreme communicators with the license to use God's Word with authority and power.

This is true because Adam was given power to "name" every creature and animal. He was given power to "call things" or make heaven's sound with authoritative power to put earth's kingdoms in place.

What I am saying is that prayer restores us to our communication power that even the earth will respond to when we choose to walk in it. Prayer was always designed for us to be able to rule over planet earth. Again it is ruling power for the human to exercise his legal right as the sole inheritor of planet earth. Are you ready to start ruling more?

Earth really is your inheritance, but it says *asking of Him*. By asking He means prayer, and by prayer He means His language system and sound. God literally says if we will make His sound and communicate with Him on that level again, He will restore our birth right inheritance.

One of the reasons the earth is your inheritance is because it operates on sound just like you do. Remember sound is energy traveling through channels of frequency called wavelengths. Earth is one big wavelength and so are you. This means the law of sound governs everything. That's why Jesus could speak to trees, dead bodies, and even loaves of bread and dead fish. Why? He exercised His ruling dominion to take back earth's inheritance by making the right sound. Jesus leveraged those divine laws of sound to perpetuate miracle after miracle.

Jesus gave that same praying authority back to you. You have to notice that not one time does Jesus ever pray in the form of asking God. He always stated His demands and left. Whether it was healing the sick or speaking to storms He always made demands, not requests.

He was operating in the dimension and law of knocking. Applying spiritual law through divine communication to produce the dominion of sound over all creation. We have that same ability now through the cross. Right now you can leverage the power of sound to create turn around in any season you desire. It's time to possess your inheritance.

Praying is therefore a high subconscious act involving the dynamics of spiritual law, creational law and natural law. God moves through sound and uses its laws to produce total victory in our lives.

God says you are His child; that means you have divine access to your royal inheritance. Leverage the law of sound to divinely communicate your rights as a ruling heir to planet earth.

The earth will respond as it is designed through the laws of attraction to bring to you whatever you desire. However, creation is crying out for the "sons of God," those who know how to make the sound of heaven by reclaiming their royal rights of sonship and inheritance.

Remember to continue charging up a powerful paradigm of praying by adding this concept to your thoughts: *My inheritance of sonship is released through my divine communication. I can literally possess the earth by agreeing with God's sound and reproducing it in the earth.* Leverage the supreme subconscious act of prayer to possess your inheritance of planet earth.

Power Concepts from this Chapter

❖ The major mark of seasoned maturity is one's ability to control their tongue.

❖ When you value your words, you begin to alter your mindset and make conscious decisions to become a steward of your mouth.

❖ Prayer is not about what we can accomplish. It's about God strategically using our words as channels of power to release His Kingdom into the earth.

❖ The power to produce and manifest our greatest desires is a natural function of Kingdom powered praying.

❖ You are raised and seated with Christ in heavenly realms.

❖ Praying from your power seat empowers you to view seemingly big challenges for what they are by holding those circumstances up against the complete authority of God's hand.

The Ultimate Secrets to Answered Prayer

9

The Bidding War

Every year millions of businesses place their bids for government contracts. Regardless of how big or small, or how young or old, every company is given a fair shot to win the bid to be providers of service for government needs. In the same token there is a constant bidding war taking place for your tongue. And the two main contractors are God's Blessing and the Babylonian Kingdom.

Though many people do not realize it, Satan is as much as a foreign ruler to planet earth as God is. However, when the scripture calls him the ruler of the air or makes common references to him having dominion in the earth, it's only referencing the fact that as of right now, he has the majority of the bidding contracts in the earth.

However, God has a plan to bring His church into a mature understanding as to how His government functions so that the kingdoms of the earth will most certainly become the kingdoms of our God. Nevertheless, we as heavenly diplomats have the responsibility to continue producing God's sound in the earth to ensure that the Kingdom of God has the winning bid for our life. You see, as I mentioned before, the earth is a government ruled by the kingdom of humans.

Regardless of how it may seem, man is still the dominant kingdom in the earth as designed by God, and the spiritual kingdom can only influence this earth through the contract of our words. When we as humans choose to make the sound of heaven, we have awarded the contract of *life* to manifest in this earth. Likewise, when we choose to speak out of alignment with God's Word we are contracting another kingdom to rule and influence the systems of this world.

One of the reasons the church has been behind is because the enemy has understood that prayer is a language and continues to influence humans with his sound through various methods. The church on the other hand has limited prayer to an act of self-effort that only happens when we are doing it. Therefore, we don't see the significance in speaking God's Word all the time and influencing the kingdoms of this earth with that sound. Every day there is a bidding war for your tongue, and you get to choose who gets the contract. Remember that when companies bid, it's not about who's the biggest or most experienced; it all comes down to who wins the contract. Because whoever wins the contract wins the influence, and that kingdom will manifest in our lives and in this world.

We are literally tied to an agreement through the sound we make, and this is the major cause for what shows up in our life, whether Blessing or curse. I remember becoming frustrated over the idea of Satan ruling in the same place God is trying to rule.

Sometimes it can seem as though Satan somehow has the power to contend with God's Kingdom. This is not so. However, God spoke to me one night about this and told me, "It's not about who's kingdom is the strongest, it's about who wins the bidding war."

So although God's Kingdom is the most supreme sound and authority that exists, if we don't agree with it, it will have no effect on us. This is the power of God's plan for divine diplomacy through the foreign aid of His royal citizenship in the earth, the church. Your prayers literally empower the invisible and the intangible to take manifestation when the kingdom laws of communication are operated correctly.

Heaven's Fair Act Policy

By now you've probably realized something about God, who is the King of all creation. He is fair and He is just. The Bible talks about God's justness and His commitment to ruling with fairness in all affairs. Although heaven is the sovereign world power, God has put into effect policies that even He Himself must honor according to His own words. This powerful truth is found in Psalm 138:2 (AMP):

> *For You have exalted above all else Your name and Your word and You have magnified Your word above all Your name!*

God is just and has even made Himself subject to the promises and policies of His Word. Such policies include man's right to choose which kingdom he will serve and which system he will operate in, without the interference or interruption of anyone else. Now look at this scripture verse below:

> *See I have set before you this day, Life or Death, Blessing or Curse.*

> Deuteronomy 30:15 (KJV)

Remember the system of *life* and the system of *death* both spring forth in our lives through the sound of our tongue (Proverbs 18:21). Believe it or not, this is a part of what I like to call "Heaven's Fair Act Policy." In short, God has made it clear through His word that His policy concerning mankind is the free will to choose his own destiny. Although it is His good pleasure to see us prosper through His original design for us, this is all contingent on the basis of us choosing to agree with that plan through the signature power and contract life of our tongues.

That's how we sign the contract of *life* and determine which government will rule over us. Romans 10:10 reminds us that with our hearts we agree with God's sound, but with our mouths we justify His words to become our authority and reality. God wants you to understand that your destiny is your decision. It always has been and you have the promise of God's fair act policy to choose Blessing or curse by the contract you award for the bidding of your tongue. It's important to understand these operations of Blessing. Jesus paid the ultimate price for sin. He positioned us for favor, blessing and unlimited breakthrough by empowering us with His Kingdom.

However, we have to understand how to benefit from these blessings now. God has done everything He will ever need to do to bless us, but as individuals ruling in another kingdom we have to learn how to bring God's promises and provision to pass in our life through the power of agreement.

Understanding your right to choose will empower you that you can actually control your life. I don't know about you but it's good news to me to know that I have the right to determine what happens in my own life. That's fair and that's just. See, you can leverage the power of God's fairness policy to speak heaven's language over every situation and communicate frequencies that empower God's will in your life.

And once you have agreed and determined that God's Kingdom will be the sole governing force and sound in your life, no one has the right to interrupt or interfere with that. It's a Kingdom policy that can't be undone or overturned!

No matter how things may seem, you can have confidence in God's Word and its ability to bring you through, knowing your tongue has shaped an agreement of Blessing whose contract life will not expire. You are in position to reap positive outcomes according to heaven's fair act policy. You choose who wins the bidding war of your tongue.

The Power of the Preceding Word

No matter how things may appear to our natural eye and our five senses, God is always saying something about our lives and us. He is always ready to reveal something He has already done and is ready to manifests in our lives.

He's waiting on our agreement, not just with what He said, but what He is saying right now. At this very moment, you are a candidate for heavenly influence. There are things God wants to show you and tell you right now that can better your life if you can believe it and receive it. Prayer is not only designed to express God's will through us, but to remind us of His contagious love and undying desire to commune with us at any given time. You see, His thoughts are constantly good towards us and those thoughts are to give us hope and a prosperous outcome.

It's God's desire that those thoughts become an internal guide for the purpose navigating us with His Word so that we are always positioned to be empowered by His will. When we are led by another source in our daily life, it's hard to shift gears and become tuned by God's internal navigation just when we pray.

So, it becomes imperative that tuning our heart to God's sound or His Word becomes our major priority as Kingdom citizens. We need to be inspired by God's will all the time, not only when making supplication to Him. If we can grasp this we will place greater value on the preceding word from God's mouth about the situations of our life. Without that value our communication with God will fade, because although we are redeemed, faith or empowered living comes by hearing and hearing of the Word of God. Referring back to John 8, Jesus makes it clear that His testimony of Himself was only powered by what God was already saying.

What is God saying about you right now? What He is saying is what He's thinking. What He is thinking and those thoughts should be the gage of our internal compass. Jesus expressed that God 'sent' Him based on what He was told. His movements and actions were tuned by His hearing of God's preceding Word.

This is how life is designed to function in the Kingdom. He goes further to explain (v.42) that people cannot understand His language if they don't have the same perceptions as Him. Again, this makes reference to our ability to hear. Well, remember that faith or life in the Blessing comes by hearing, or perception.

That perception, Jesus proposes, produces His language. When individuals don't speak His language He says they belong to another kingdom (v.44). God is not saying that He is denying or rejecting us; we are under grace. Yet, He certainly isn't going to endorse a language system that isn't His. So if we pray need and fear-based prayers, we are being snared by the language accent of Babylon.

Jesus said, "Whoever belongs to God hears what He says" (v.47). The mark of citizenship in the Kingdom is our ability to hear what God is saying. Again, the righteous live by faith and that faith comes by hearing God's Word. So in order to power up God's preceding Word we need to train our ears to His written words.

Every day we should be confessing and declaring the Word of God from the scriptures to empower our thoughts for the day. This is the foundation of clear Kingdom communication and Kingdom praying. The written words of God allow us to turn our hearts to God's sound. This opens us up for more heavenly communication. Since the written Word is flowing from God's thoughts we can leverage His words to create faith-filled, God inspired confessions.

This is how we really get the Kingdom laws of prayer operating in our lives. If we can learn to value the written words of God, He will speak His preceding word to us so we can hear and perceive what we should channel through our words into this earth. Speaking the will of God is a level of prayer mastery. However, we must understand that highly esteemed value for the Word of God is what releases the preceding word from God specifically concerning your situation.

Our confession based on what God has said becomes inspired by His will, not ours. This makes our words and daily declarations valid to release His authority. Sometimes our confession is the only solution to possessing a harvest. We need an instruction from God many times, so it's important to understand that daily confession also acts as a preparation for the heart to receive God's commands. As we become the command center for God's heart, He gives us revelation allowing us into His plan and what steps we need to take to produce a harvest.

Nevertheless, God has a plan and it always works when we trust Him. Our citizenship gives us the natural born right to hear God; it's one of our spiritual 5 senses. The same way we hear physically, we have an internal ear that can pick up God's frequency and relay clear messages through His Spirit in us.

That's why: "man cannot live by bread alone, but by every word that proceeds from the mouth of God" (Matthew 4:4). When Jesus was led into the wilderness and tempted by Satan, He was challenged to turn stone into bread to eat. Though Jesus was hungry He would not acknowledge His hunger because it was an indication of lack or need.

Jesus came to restore the Blessing where needs are met and provision is supplied. So if He would have placed His physical need over His spiritual state then it would've been like Adam bowing to the Babylonian government all over again.

You see, Babylon trains individuals to serve their natural senses over their spiritual ones. Instead, Jesus spoke the written words of God to discern the spirit He was hearing. Those written words became His proceeding words as He eventually made the right confession that brought forth His breakthrough.

Jesus leveraged the bread (written words) to produce a proceeding Word from God's mouth, and it led to supernatural invasion. Angels came to attend to Jesus because of His firm stand to allow God's sound to be His navigation source. So man shall not live by bread *alone*, but also by the very words coming from God's mouth.

Those words are a navigation source that will lead us down paths of prosperity and blessings, but only as they guide our tongues first. I am telling you that when we place value on God's written words, then God will supply us with a proceeding word to direct us into unlimited favor and breakthrough.

It's time to make sure you are examining closely: What's your value of the written Word? Do you see how placing a greater value on God's written words can influence your overall prayer life? See, when we confess the Word, we are still praying. Remember that prayer is a language system with many different forms of communication. Word confessions produce proceeding words from God as our value increases daily to cover all we do with the words of God.

You can be sure that God is automatically joined to your situation and the outcome as you have cultivated it with His sound. Soon enough, God's going to place other things in your heart to say and do that will bring about full manifestation.

I want to encourage you to be sure that you purchase the other prayer books in this series to go along with *"The Prayer Paradigm."* These resources are designed to propel your prayer life and coach you into the proper way to decree the Word and establish God's Blessing in your life.

Every area of your life can be spiritual jurisdictions of God's favor and mercy when you leverage His written words to produce a proceeding word into to the command center of your heart. And from your heart the word will travel to the pathway of your tongue and into this earth realm as an unbreakable contract of *life*.

The Material Covenant

God's written words are just as valuable as His proceeding words. In fact, they both are proceeding words at some point. What I want to direct your attention to is the function of both as two different evidences of a two-sided covenant Blessing that exists for us as citizens of the covenant Kingdom.

The land in the earth is material substance for us to live out the Kingdom mandate and rule in. This would represent the covenant blessing of bread and the words of life that are written.

These words are written as covenant keys to give us access into the material Blessing of Abraham, Isaac, and Jacob. They are keys that unlock the words of life spoken as proceeding words. In this sense, the written words are the bread, access keys to the material covenant.

Now, in this sense of I am referring to the promises of God already written in His Word called the Bible. These are written promises, and from the old testament to the new testament over 8,000 promises exist as prewritten key codes or "secrets" that will unleash a manifestation of substance material Blessing in the earth realm.

You have to remember that the covenant of Blessing is two-sided and when you entered into the Kingdom you received both sides.

Now, as the bread represents the earth and the material contract of Abraham, the wine makes reference to the spiritual Blessing and covenant made with Christ. The covenant Blessings of the Kingdom are entry points into manifestation of inheritance of God's children.

We get the material covenant through Abraham and our rights to spiritual Blessing through Christ. Just as Christ sat at the table with His disciples for His last meal with them He broke bread symbolizing the Abrahamic covenant and He drank wine symbolizing the spiritual covenant that was bought with His blood. He made it clear that faith in Him was now the beginning point of each Blessing. Though we are seeds of Abraham we are now brothers with Jesus and sons of the living God.

So the beginning point of each covenant now is marked with the blood of Jesus and our faith in sacrifice. From here we acknowledge who the covenant came through in regards to its original inheritor in the earth. The material abundance of Abraham is a contract from God to bless us with substantial blessing, financial increase, and every physical blessing you can think of. This came through Abraham's faith but Jesus' blood activates this covenant. So, in Christ we have access to tangible blessings but also there are spiritual blessings. Ephesians 1:3 (AMP) says:

> *May blessing (praise, laudation, and eulogy) be to the God and Father of our Lord Jesus Christ (the Messiah) Who has blessed us in Christ with every spiritual (given by the Holy Spirit) blessing in the heavenly realm!*

Our spiritual blessings in Christ come through the Holy Spirit and we receive them by faith in Jesus and His Kingdom. Now, those spiritual blessings include: prophetic gifting, spiritual signs, revelation knowledge, other spiritual gifts, and of course eternal life.

Through Christ we inherit the richest blessing of all which is restoration to the divine position of Kingdom citizenship with the inherited right to constant relationship and interaction with the

King. Many people in church remain stuck at this Blessing and fail to realize that the Blessing of God's Kingdom has two sides to it. It's the spiritual and material Blessing.

Now again, the bread represents that material covenant with Abraham in this sense of food. This also makes reference to the written words of God, which become keys that unlock our inheritance of material promises already given in scripture. Without faith in the written promises of God you can't release the tangible substance of material Blessing. These promises are the bread or earthy provision of God.

When the bread was offered to Jesus on the mountain as a temptation from Satan to change it from a stone, He was being asked to take one kingdom and put it over the other. The stone in this case represents revelation knowledge. You may refer back to the well-known story of Peter's confession of Jesus as Christ. In that same story Jesus called Peter "rock" and said that on that rock (revelation knowledge) He would build His church. Well, remember that revelation knowledge is one of the main spiritual blessings of Christ's spiritual covenant.

So again, He was being tempted to misappropriate kingdoms of blessings. The enemy wanted Jesus to do what a lot of Christians actually find themselves doing when seeking and praying to God. They put their physical blessing or needs over the spiritual ones. And as I stated before when we serve our 5 senses over our spiritual ones it's the same as Adam bowing to the Babylonian kingdom all over again.

Why? Because Babylon is an earthly kingdom that possesses no spiritual inheritance. It's a kingdom based in earth, ruled by earth and only substantiated by earth. Though Satan's government of darkness governs it, Babylon still takes its root in the earth realm as a kingdom of flesh, human need, and want with no regard for the spiritual things of life. You see, bread is good, but if we allow it to control our life we will take the stone (spiritual blessings) and turn it into bread (material blessings). We will misinterpret God's purpose for prosperity in the earth and begin to chase after human need instead of spiritual things. This is how need-based praying comes takes life. When the bread is misappropriated and placed over the wine we lose the spiritual power of Christ's covenant to release any blessing to us as God desires. Our physical needs are not the priority, the spiritual blessing of Christ is.

That spiritual blessing is the covenant of the Kingdom of God. So when Jesus warns us in Luke 12 not to worry and pray about food, need or clothing He's referencing His experience in the desert as an apostolic mandate for all kingdom citizens to follow. He literally tells them to seek first the Kingdom of God, or the spiritual covenant of Blessing.

He said don't worry about these things of the flesh (carnal kingdom) because the pagans run after such things. We are not pagans; we are a community of citizens with covenant blessings. In other words, when we pray need over spiritual blessing, we negate His covenant and place physical need over God's Kingdom.

This is praying Babylonian and allowing need and want to rule your prayers. God didn't say pray about needs. He said ask what you desire, because I want to fulfill it for you. God's wants to prosper you beyond your wildest dreams both tangible and spiritually, but you have to return to a Kingdom covenant mindset. That material blessing of Abraham is good, but it becomes a snare to believers when we pray about need and things of the earth's nature over our complete spiritual state as God-beings with every need supplied according to His riches and glory.

You have to ask yourself, what will it be for you? Are you going to continue to pray Babylonian? God already knows your need; don't be tempted to turn the stone into bread. Don't trade your spiritual blessing, which is your redeemed state as a born again citizen of the Kingdom, for the material blessings. You can have both because you inherited both.

In this way, that material earthly substance becomes the material kingdom of God reigning and at work in your life. You will see a tangible explosion as you pray from the paradigm of "needs met" according to the abundant provision of God's Eden plan. You are restored to this same covenant and the Blessing is on you. Our words and how we pray play a major part in whether or not the Blessing is released in fullness.

The Covenant Kingdom of God

Now again the Kingdom of God is the Kingdom of Blessing, both material and spiritual. God has made a contract to bless you in the earth realm with exceeding abundance of riches and prosperity, but He has established with it the spiritual Blessing of Jesus Christ.

Referencing back to the final supper, in which Jesus partook of dinner with His disciples in the form of bread and wine, He was establishing new connection points between the Blessing of Abraham and the Blessing of the Holy Spirit. Notice that when He does this He does it with them while sitting at the table. They are in communion with one another, seated next to each other fellowshipping together.

They are in one place, in one setting at the same time, all eating the same thing. This is rather important when it comes to the internalization and materialization of God's Blessing through prayer.

When Jesus calls them to the "upper room" it represents a new dimension, a spiritual place. In the same way, prayer is that dimension we enter into to seek the place of intimate communion with God.

It is at the spiritual table of fellowship that we connect to favor and covenant blessings; it's all at the table. So when Jesus communes with them at the table He broke the bread and ate it, and did also the same with wine to represent the double portion of

Blessing He had been made a steward of. He said in order to fellowship with Him at this table of covenant Blessing we'd have to do so with understanding of the Kingdom of God. Now look at these scripture verses:

> *For I say to you, I shall eat it no more until it is fulfilled in the kingdom of God...For I say to you that from now on I shall not drink of the fruit of the vine at all until the kingdom of God comes...This cup is the new testament or covenant [ratified] in My blood, which is shed (poured out) for you.*

Luke 22:16-20 (AMP)

The word *fulfilled* here in the Greek means "to fully understand or to have complete understanding" as in revelation knowledge. I also want to point out that Jesus calls this the New Testament or "Covenant" because *covenant* is the literal Greek word for *testament*. So really He states this is the "New Covenant." Notice now, He says "in my blood" is the starting point or connection place to where this new covenant begins.

Jesus is plainly stating that understanding the Kingdom of God is now going to be the only way we commune and dine with Him at the table of Blessing, bread and wine. That's the spiritual and material Kingdom of God. This scripture was not telling us to begin a ritual.

It was teaching us to understand that we cannot eat and drink or have commune fellowship with God except by coming into the Kingdom paradigm of understanding, and there, fulfillment will come as we discover the body and blood in us. This understanding makes our hearts the proper meeting grounds for continual fellowship with God as we dine with Him through revelation as to how we operate in the Kingdom of God, mainly the higher dimension of the law of prayer.

God's system of communication is the place of continual fellowship when we pray with revelation and operate prayer correctly. So, by doing this Jesus is claiming His legal right as the beneficiary of Abraham's contract of material blessing. You see, although Abraham became the father of the material covenant of blessing, He was also given rights to the spiritual blessing as well, which all came by faith.

He doesn't manifest the spiritual blessing because it belongs to His seed, which is Jesus Christ, the true redeemer of mankind and the original Son and beneficiary to every thing and every blessing God has.

However, Abraham did accept the full license to that covenant Blessing from Melchizedek in Genesis 13. Where did that Blessing come from before Melchizedek? It was from Adam. Adam was the original beneficiary to every earthly blessing and spiritual blessing. So, when Adam forfeited the Kingdom he lost those rights to the Blessing and God was waiting for Abraham, a man, to show up with faith in order to redeem those covenants rights to man and reactivate His Blessing.

Now, when Abraham meets with Melchizedek to inherit this Blessing notice he meets Melchizedek in a valley. This also represents a higher dimension as in a spiritual place, just like an upper room does.

Notice the resemblances between the encounters of Jesus at the table with His disciples teaching on the Blessing with bread and wine and also Abraham's encounter with Melchizedek at the table eating bread and wine with Melchizedek. Let's take a look closer now at Genesis 13:

> *After his [Abram's] return from the defeat and slaying of*
> *Chedorlaomer and the kings who were with him, the king*

of Sodom went out to meet him at the Valley of Shaveh, that is, the King's Valley. Melchizedek king of Salem [later called Jerusalem] brought out bread and wine [for their nourishment]; he was the priest of God Most High, And he blessed him and said, Blessed (favored with blessings, made blissful, joyful) be Abram by God Most High, Possessor and Maker of heaven and earth And blessed, praised, and glorified be God Most High, Who has given your foes into your hand! And [Abram] gave him a tenth of all [he had taken].

Genesis 13:17-20 (AMP)

So, here we see that Abraham's encounter with Melchizedek models exactly Jesus' fellowship with His disciples at the last supper. In fact, to take this further, you'll notice the amplified version points out that the valley Abraham met Melchizedek in is called *Shaveh*, which means kings. Now take into account that Jesus is the King of the Jews and He is sitting at the table with His disciples offering a Blessing covenant through relationship of fellowship communion through understanding of a Kingdom paradigm of prayer (communication).

Melchizedek's name means "King of Salem" (as in Jerusalem). Now both scenarios take place at the table with kings and in each scenario communion is partaken with bread and wine. Why? Because this represents earthly inheritance (bread) and spiritual inheritance (wine).

So in other words, both the disciples and Abraham are seated at the table of covenant fellowship called the place of kings. I want to pause briefly to point out that this is a perfect picture of the powerful covenant fellowship we have with God as royal princes and His royal priesthood seated at the table of fellowship called prayer. Here we connect to all spiritual and material blessing by confessing the written words of God and receiving the proceeding words from His Spirit.

We have returned to the same realm of anointing and influence through the supreme nature of the God-life in us restored through the royal blood of Jesus Christ. You are seated in the place of kings. Leverage prayer properly to access this continual fellowship within your inner being. This what the scriptures mean by, "We have been raised and seated with Christ in heavenly realms."

Your governing seat takes place at the table of continual covenant fellowship marked by faith in Jesus and an understanding of how to successfully operate the laws of heavenly communication through a Kingdom paradigm of prayer. So, although Abraham and the disciples existed at two different times, they still had access to the same promise. Just as you and I still have access to them today.

Furthermore, Abraham is named possessor of heaven and earth, which again means the possessor of the spiritual blessing and material blessing. Heaven is the wine and the bread is equal to the earth realm. We are kings in heaven with ruling authority and power in the earth.

We must leverage the principles of gaining wisdom concerning the Kingdom to unlock this powerful Blessing of God. One of the ways we do this begins with grabbing the keys to bread or material blessing that will unlock earthly inheritance, which are the written promises of God.

I cannot express how important it is that we learn to apply the promises written in the Bible, because those written words unlock those written promises. I'll explain it like this. You need the right key to open the right door. Since all tangible release for whatever we possess as legal inheritors of the Kingdom is consistent with how we "ask" or operate the language of heaven, we can't afford to be "off" with our sound.

So, when Peter gained the right revelation of Jesus as the

Son of God, Jesus promised Him something valuable in Matthew 16:19 (AMP):

> *I will give you the keys of the kingdom of heaven; and whatever you bind (declare to be improper and unlawful) on earth must be what is already bound in heaven; and whatever you loose (declare lawful) on earth must be what is already loosed in heaven.*

You have to realize that, again, the reference of heaven and earth falls in exact alignment with both encounters of the disciples at dinner with Jesus and Melchizedek's offering to Abraham.

Furthermore, the principle of spiritual blessing is represented, heaven, and the principle of material blessing is acknowledged as earth. So, the keys to the Kingdom, which represent doors and access, are of two kinds, heavenly authority and earthly authority.

It's because the Blessing we've inherited has given us spiritual dominion as well as earthly dominion. Also, we cannot fail to point out that this scripture states that the way these keys operate is whenever one *declares* something lawful or *declares* it unlawful. So, declaration power as we discussed is a form of prayer, which Jesus clearly proposes, are powerful keys for releasing spiritual inheritance along with our material inheritance. Now, let's tie all three encounters together:

Abraham receives the Blessing from the king through a fellowship encounter of bread and wine, which are the two forms of the covenant Blessing. From that time on, he possessed the power and authority (keys) to walk in supernatural wealth and obtain earthly riches without any strife, deficit or decline. In the same way, Jesus, the King, invites the disciples to the fellowship table with Him concerning the new covenant offered in bread and wine. The disciples are receiving covenant power (keys) again to unlock supernatural manifestation of a powerful blessing on a spiritual and material level as we witness throughout their ministry.

Finally Peter taps into the correct revelation and declares (sound) that Jesus is the Messiah. Immediately Jesus *blesses* him (empowerment) and gives him the keys to manifest the Kingdom in heaven and earth by simply declaring something lawful or unlawful as an expression of the administrative power of the spiritual and material Kingdom of God at work in us. As citizens of this divine government we possess power and authority through declaration or sound, which become keys that unlock material promises of God as well as spiritual promises.

Table Talking

So indeed we are in the valley of kings and we are sitting at the King's table in continual communion and fellowship with the King. He's agreed with us and offered us a double portion of Blessing to manifest earthly inheritance through our power seat or spiritual substance by making the right sound. Our prayer power flows from revelation of the Kingdom of God where the communion place of covenant fellowship is fulfilled in us. We are disciples of Jesus and seeds of Abraham, honorary beneficiaries of a two-sided covenant Blessing.

However, when praying material need over our spiritual senses we misappropriate the Kingdom of God and fall victim to a government system of need-based thinking and asking. Remember you are at the King's table and have access to all the bread you want.

That is why the scripture says, "*I have been young and now am old, yet have I not seen the [uncompromisingly] righteous forsaken or their seed begging for bread.* (Psalm 37:25 AMP.) Well, think about it, if you're sitting at the table where the food is you don't have to beg for it. You don't have to keep repeating yourself saying, "Pass the bread...pass the bread!" You don't even have to yell, you can simply look at your father who is sitting at the table with you and say, "Pass the bread."

Well, isn't that what Jesus does when He demonstrates high impact praying in the Lord's Prayer? "Give us our daily bread." He doesn't yell or beg; He operates in the Kingdom paradigm of prayer, understanding that He's already at the table and material blessings are His through the right declaration (key.)

The same goes for you. You are sitting at the table of covenant blessing, so don't chase after bread. Instead, acknowledge who God is, take a bold stance to concentrate on how your needs are met, and pray with this confident state of constant provision and wholeness. Resist the temptation to turn stone into bread; be like Jesus and respond back to the negative sound of need: *"man shall not live by bread alone, but by every word that proceeds out the mouth of God."*

Leverage your faith and your power position of communion fellowship at your Father's table to remain covenant-minded. In doing so you will be able to release covenant blessings with the right declarations from the written promises of God. Those written promises are faith infused keys, which will unlock the tangible inheritance of the Kingdom of God's material purpose in your life.

The ultimate secret to answered prayer is remembering that there is a bidding war for your tongue and the contractor is one sound away. It's also remembering that the proceeding word of God flows from the power of confessing the written Word. This is how you put together the blessing of spiritual and material promise: positioning yourself to receive a real deposit from God. God wants us to know that the secret to staying on His communication system is always speaking the promises of the Word. By doing this you're creating an atmosphere perpetually influenced by the sound waves of heaven.

It's time to declare your spiritual promises of life, authority and divine dominion. But don't limit yourself to just spiritual promises. Gain your favor position in the kingdoms of this life by lawfully declaring written promises from the written Word to unlock an inheritance of material abundance, financial gain, and unlimited benefits.

You are favor. You are the righteousness of God, and blessings crown the head of the righteous. Take your seat at the communion table of fellowship and continue in covenant Blessing as you feast on the inheritance of promise through the power of a prayer paradigm.

Power Concepts from this Chapter

- ❖ There are 2 kingdoms bidding for your tongue. You can decide who wins the bidding contract by choosing to speak God's sound.
- ❖ Every time you make the sound of heaven you award the bidding contract of *life* to manifest in this earth.
- ❖ God is just and has even made Himself subject to the promises and policies of His Word. Such policies include man's right to choose which kingdom he will serve and which system he will operate in.
- ❖ God's plan is always to prosper you, but you must agree with that plan through the signature power and contract life of your words.
- ❖ No matter how things may appear to our natural eye and our five senses, God is always saying something about us and our lives.
- ❖ Word confessions produce proceeding words from God as our value increases daily to cover all we do with words of God.
- ❖ The ultimate secret to answered prayer is remembering that there is a bidding war for your tongue and the contractor is one sound away.

The Empowered Language of God's Blessing

10

The Language of Babble

As citizens of a new country we must learn to adapt to our culture so that it becomes a daily expression of our life. Language is evidence of which kingdom we are operating in. It doesn't mean that we haven't switched kingdoms if we are not operating in kingdom culture and language; Jesus translated us into His government and nothing can change that. However, our language system controls how much of the Kingdom system actually shows up in our life. We are still the human kingdom; therefore, our constant agreement and alignment with heaven's communication will be a determinate factor of which system influences our reality.

It's easy to tell what country someone is from by his or her native language. Language reveals the culture and nation prevalent in a person's life. For example, whenever I am traveling and I meet people with different accents foreign to the place they live in I always try to guess their country. The more I travel and the more languages I encounter the better I am getting. Now I am able to tell which part of the world certain people are from simply by hearing their accent. So, although they may be speaking a different language, the accent of their previous language is still influencing how they speak and communicate.

It's no different with learning to communicate the Kingdom of God's way. Whether we realize it or not, heaven is a new country for us so it's not unlikely for traces of the Babylonian language to show up in our communication, especially when we pray. That language of Babylon is call *"babble."*

This is a major issue concerning prayer, not only in our personal lives but also in the church as a whole. Many teachings coach and encourage this language system under the impression that God hears our prayer the more we repeat ourselves.

Though this may sound right, biblically it's simply not true. Wordiness is never a way to get our prayers heard or to communicate with heaven. Babbling is the mark of a person whose accent and language are still being influenced by a kingdom and culture that is outside of God's Blessing.

Remember, prayer is our language system and it's based on the divine law system of sound. All of creation functions based on sound and without the right inspiration to our sound, it can be responsible for a whole lot of things happening to us that God never intended. You have to remember that no matter what, the Blessing of the Lord brings wealth and adds no troubles (sorrow) with it (Proverbs 10:22).

God doesn't bring sorrow of any kind. I realize how difficult this may be for the average Christian to accept, but we must place God back into His proper perspective and realize that when His Kingdom has been fully cultivated in a person's life, His language systems will produce sound waves that manifest heaven's prosperity beyond any limits we can imagine.

However, when our language is being influenced by Babylonian sounds, the bidding war for our tongue is still going to the wrong contractor. This causes the benefits of the Blessing to be constrained as traces of the Babylonian culture keep showing up and dominating the lives of Christians. That's why we have to start with our prayer life, how we communicate with God, and commit to wiping out every trace of sorrowful praying. This includes wordiness. This wordy style of prayer is not God-endorsed, nor is it a Kingdom model for prayer. Based on the Kingdom principles that Jesus taught, He never encouraged us to pray this way.

In fact, Jesus was against praying wordy prayers and gave warning signals to His disciples that Kingdom citizens should not pray this way. This kind of praying only creates exhaustion and confusion along with the frustration of unanswered prayer. Look at this scripture passage in Matthew 6:7-8:

> *And when you pray, do not keep on babbling like pagans, for they think they will be heard because of their many words. Do not be like them, for your Father knows what you need before you ask him.*

Wordiness is the language of another kingdom that is why Jesus calls those whose pray like this "pagans." The very heart of what Jesus is saying aims to express the operation of another language and kingdom. Pagan, by the way, literally means "people outside of the (Jewish) covenant community."

This indicates a different system or culture versus the covenant Blessing system and how it operates. So, here Jesus is teaching the laws of prayer, how they function and the best way to get results with them. He is clear that wordy praying is not the culture of the Kingdom of God. Yet, many people around the world have the belief system that the more we say, the more God will do. We have to move beyond this idea because it's not empowered by the Blessing system of God.

Notice that Jesus links wordy praying to individuals who function in the mindset that *"they will be heard."* This is one of the root conditions of a babbling heart: not believing that you *"have been heard."* When Jesus says, *"they think,"* He is referring to a paradigm that many believers operate in concerning prayer. Some of us are convinced that we will be heard if we pray enough hours and say certain things enough times. However, this kind of praying only incites the Babylonian influence because it isn't the language system of heaven. Therefore, when we pray this way, regardless of what *we think*, we will not *be heard*.

So, again we can dispel the mistruth floating around concerning prayer that God hears every prayer. As Jesus is proposing, we may think we will be heard, but unless we pray according to His Kingdom model we will not see results.

In reality, when we speak another language system, we are opening the door for another kingdom to come in and "add sorrow" to our lives. I am telling you this is a major entry point for a lot of negativity flowing into Christians' lives. Many people sow spiritual warfare in prayer and as a result are in a constant reaping mode of endless "battles" with the devil. The Kingdom paradigm comes to eradicate that sorrowful mentality that the battle isn't already won.

We triumphed through Christ's blood and the word of our testimony. This means our "testimony" is valid as in our confession based on the agreement of two: the Holy Spirit and us. When we learn the power of covenant agreement with God and His Blessing system we are no longer to pray from a laborious and defeated mentality. There is no sense in fighting an enemy who is already defeated.

On the contrary, when the Blessing system is operating through the pathway of our tongues, we will invite life, and the perfect picture of peace and rest will overcome the sorrowful burden of a laborious prayer mentality. This peaceful rest will become a constant stream in the heart of Kingdom citizens who are fully cultivating their new language. Again, this Kingdom paradigm of praying is an enriched and effective approach to gaining real success with our petitions to God.

Breaking Free From Babylonian Praying
Now, let's add another scripture to this point:

> *Guard your steps when you go to the house of God. Go near to listen rather than to offer the sacrifice of fools, who do not know that they do wrong. Do not be quick with your mouth; do not be hasty in your heart to utter anything before God. God is in heaven and you are on earth, so let your words be few. A dream comes when there are many cares, and many words mark the speech of a fool.*

> Ecclesiastes 5:1-3

The starting point for a successful prayer life begins at the place we discover God's original intent for prayer. It is His language system designed to communicate with Him for the purposes of translating His sound and purpose to us and through us in the earth. When we take prayer out of its original design and Kingdom context we become accustomed to traditions and form habits that God didn't teach us. We become self-imposed about how the systems of the Kingdom should operate and we find ourselves snared by the trip wire of misunderstanding.

Prayer was designed for us to receive a genuine download from God as we listen to His heart and clearly communicate that sound in the earth realm for manifestation. This is why we cannot afford to babble when we pray. We are allowing traces of another language to influence our accent so the sound of heaven is corrupted through our mouth. We are the passageways for all tangible Kingdom expression in this world. But as the scripture establishes, we cannot be hasty with words and expect a real response from God. We have to change communication systems and allow God to produce His sound through us and into this earth realm.

Now take also into account these words in Proverbs 10:8:

The wise in heart accept commands, but a chattering fool comes to ruin.

We all know what it's like to feel the need to be wordy with our prayers. We have to be secure enough to confront the bad beliefs we've held onto in order to exchange them with the right truth and create successful turnaround. When we look at God's perspective in this verse, He says our hearts are designed to receive command and instruction. This literally means that the heart is the command center for Kingdom communication. A wise heart, one that is governed by the principles of God's Word, is more likely to receive instruction than produce wordiness that is uninspired by God.

This falls into the principle of listening that we discussed earlier in chapter 3. Listening offsets babbling and is inspired by the power of trust. Trust equals security and as Jesus proposes in Matthew 6, individuals only pray needy prayers when they don't realize the Father knows their situation and already has them covered. He strategically links wordy praying and need-based petitions to individuals who operate in a paradigm outside of the Blessing mentality.

In the Blessing we recover all that Adam lost. Again, within our spirits we are redeemed and restored to the original provision plan in Eden. In Eden, God supplies all our needs, because we are His royal ambassadors, and He makes provision along with our assignment and purpose to be fulfilled. When we miss purpose, provision dries up because purpose produces provision in the Eden Blessing Plan. God hasn't changed that system, and in fact, Jesus came preaching that same Blessing only under the context of these words: the Kingdom of heaven is at hand. That same Kingdom system is the Blessing system or world order governed by Eden.

So, when we pray out of need we disconnect from the original paradigm function that God has already supplied our needs, and provision is not the responsibility of the sons. Think about this, most children don't have to worry if their parents will make provision. They don't get up asking if their needs will be met or if they will have a place to stay that night. It is the same for the children of the Kingdom of God.

Here, Jesus is practically explaining this timeless truth as not only encouragement but also an empowering factor that can dismantle the barrier of wordy need-based praying. In other words, we need to gain a clear picture of the Eden paradigm, which is based on our understanding that we are back in the Father's house and sitting at His table; He can hear us and we don't need to repeat ourselves to have real success with the language prayer system of heaven.

If we will avoid this form of repetitive praying we will be able to eliminate traces of sorrow from our lives. It has been a life changing experience to actually learn how we make ourselves a target for negative forces to invade our lives when we pray based on need and not out of a firm trust that God is using our words to simply release provision He has already stored up for us.

In essence, there are five simple keys to eliminating earth-cursed praying from your life so that the system of babble will never influence your language again:

1) Gain a clear picture of your restoration into the Adamic Blessing.
2) Build your trust in God as father, by seeing yourself as a redeemed son.

3) Allow this new paradigm of yourself to influence a bold confidence in the reality that God hears you.

4) Take a stand against wordy prayers knowing that all needs have been met through the original provision plan of the Blessing.

5) View your prayer simply as the outlet for manifesting in the earth what God has supplied through His Word.

The Language of Blessing

You know, the Blessing is a divine empowerment God has given to man in order to manifest His nature, likeness, and ability in the earth. That Blessing is the answer to any and everything out of alignment in your life. Discovering this Blessing has literally changed my life and allowed my wife and I to rise above a generational pattern of lack, poverty and limitation that has plagued both of our families for years. We have witnessed how a commitment to doing things God's way and the power of speaking in consistency with His word will manifest an unlimited design to bring you into endless prosperity.

I cannot tell you that learning these principles and how to fully tap into the God's Blessing was a walk in the park. In all actuality, I struggled for many years trying to gain results with the seed faith principle, the power of declaration, and living by faith. Like many Christians, I knew I was blessed but I didn't understand how that Blessing operated and that I had the power to release it into my life through my words. I didn't see the Blessing as an invisible provision system with the potential to take tangible form at any moment.

I came to this realization during a difficult time in my life as I was on the road traveling by faith and believing for God to open ministry doors. It seemed that no matter what path I chose, doors were always closing on me. I came to a point of great frustration and began to yell out to God about how I really felt. I wanted to know why Christians are the redeemed of God, yet struggle with getting provision met and rarely see their prayers answered. From that moment forward, He began to teach me principles of the Blessing that changed my life forever.

He showed me that though I am under grace, my way of praying and communicating was not inspired by His system. I realized that although I spoke positively and confessed the Word over certain areas of my life; it only took the right amount of pressure for me to return to a language system filled with cursing and negativity.

Truthfully I just could not see how my words about one situation could have real impact on something else I was praying and declaring over. I soon learned how sound operates and that every time I complained I threw away my confession.

It was a painful and irritating process to go through learning to change my words to line up with God's sound all the time. I had to train my tongue to stop slandering others and unconsciously speaking curses over myself. I had to put an end to laborious praying and lengthy petitions. The more I saw the picture of my perfect nature within my spirit, my heart began to line up with that picture and my words became a reflection of God's image within me. I began to approach prayer differently, thinking bolder, and speaking life even when it contradicted my emotions and feelings. I let go of Babylon's language and became empowered with the language of the Blessing, the Blessing that makes rich and adds no sorrow with it.

Essentially, I created psychological patterns of positive speech. Those patterns began to influence my words more and more. My mindset became empowered with the realization of heaven's existence within me. This helped me to discover my unlimited ability to determine outcomes, shift circumstances in my favor, and produce abundance all by disciplining my tongue to the sound waves of heaven.

I chose to no longer allow anymore bidding contracts for my tongue to be claimed by Babylon. After consistency in heaven's communication realm, supernatural blessings began to overtake my life. I am confident in the principles this book contains concerning prayer and the language of the Kingdom. They have changed my life and led me to the alarming discovery of how many Christians have the Kingdom within them, but because they lack revelation concerning the function of His internal government they continue to pray with another sound.

Nevertheless, I realized that the Blessing was being enforced through my words and a prayer life that was consistent with God's way of doing things. That Blessing emerges as a subconscious force that began to govern every area of my life. When we embrace this concept we will truly understand our ability to draw and attract blessings as well as the power to repel negativity.

Take a look at how Proverbs 10:6 paints a clear picture of how blessings flow:

> *Blessing crowns the head of the righteous, but violence overwhelms the mouth of the wicked.*

In this particular chapter, the writer of Proverbs makes many references to "the righteous" being individuals who keep their lips in alignment with the Word. He often refers to the mouth as the *way of life*. The mouth can be understood as the pathway for the system of life (Blessing) to manifest in our tangible reality. The *head of the righteous*, however, represents a strong psychological state powered by the pattern of God's language. Numerous studies have now confirmed that language is produced by a pattern in the brain, but in the same token, language can reconstruct a thought pattern through sound waves.

Those sounds release chemicals that determine our overall state as well as the atmosphere we release around us. When our tongues become the bid for God's Blessing our hearts will be transformed by the power of His supernatural empowerment. Likewise, our minds then continue to perpetuate a sound consistent with heaven's atmosphere so that tangible blessings will continue to show up and increase us.

So, simply stated, the Blessing produces a psychological state of awareness powered by the realization of one's present position as a citizen in the Kingdom of God. Our language then will follow that same pattern of that awareness as we speak the language of life, peace, and abundance over all that we think and do.

Let the crown of Blessing influence your words as you wake up the true nature of God's life within you. From the way we pray to how we communicate with others, God's Blessing should be the conductor of our words producing a clear pathway for His government to show up. You have moved on from babble. Leverage patience and the law of listening to receive and agree with God. Your agreement is the birthing place of God's sound and the fruit of all Blessing inspired by wisdom and confidence in the ability that God's language system has to bring you into total victory.

The Validation Principle

The general understanding of prayer for most people has been shaped by a self-conscious effort rather than a God-conscious one. As we examine the Bible there are numerous accounts of short and precise powerful praying that birthed some of the greatest miracles the world as ever seen. Take Elijah for example when he prayed for God to send fire to burn up the altar of Baal on Mount Carmel (1 Kings 18). He watched as this pagan community labored for hours to gain results with their lengthy prayer style. Although Christians don't pray to Baal, this is applicable for us because God's people at that time began to take on this style of praying and many began to worship Baal as well. You see, the Babylonian kingdom for years has tried to coach this same repetitive, works-oriented style of praying into our lives.

When this happens we can find ourselves trying to be heard by God by praying long hours and repeating many of the same things over and over. However, in the Kingdom prayer is not man being heard by God as many think. On the contrary, it is God being heard by man. So, God wants us to understand just what Elijah knew, that our authority in the earth realm is only validated when we pray correctly.

You see, we have been given all power and authority in heaven and earth as Jesus promised. Although this is our current state as Kingdom citizens we still need to validate who we are by manifesting God's culture in the earth. Validation produces authority, which gives us the legal right to enforce power. When we speak heaven's language and operate prayer according to God's purpose, we are validating our authority enforcing heaven on earth to create any breakthrough we desire.

Referencing back to Elijah's story (1 Kings 18:36-39), after countless hours of babbling and tireless praying to the prophets of Baal, Elijah stepped forward to demonstrate the law of prayer with a simple petition that released a major miracle. God immediately sent fire, burning the altar and sacrifice Elijah offered even after having it drenched with water four times! The resemblances of Esther, Mary and Elijah's prayer experiences reflect those of many others in the Bible that learned how to power their prayer life with God's formula for powerful effective praying.

How is it that Elijah was able to perform such an amazing miracle with such a simple yet powerful prayer? He tapped into something that God was already saying, and as a wise heart receives commands, he made his own heart the command center for God's sound. Acting on his instruction he spoke what God was already saying, charging his prayer with a confident and bold expectation.

Elijah's sound validated his authority to enforce God's will in the earth. He understood God's purpose for the matter, stating that God was using the situation to lead His people back to Him. Remember, purpose gives provision and if we can use a listening state to shift to the receiving end of prayer, God will show up and make us stewards of His Kingdom plan for divine diplomacy.

What about you today? Maybe you have some seemingly large requests that you want answered. Don't forget the unlimited power you've been given through your redeemed nature within. Leverage faith and patience to position and receive a supernatural download from God. As you connect to God's life in you, you will be inspired by His sound, His thoughts, and His perspectives.

Align with God through the joint effort of Kingdom praying. Say what He is already saying and act on His instructions. By doing this you will supernaturally empower your words with the language of heaven, which will guarantee a tangible release of miraculous outcomes for you.

The possibilities are endless as you leverage the weight of this validation principle of purpose and aligned praying into the transforming power of answered prayer. You are about to release a tangible explosion of blessings as your validation of sound along with trust in God's system and His way of doing things authorizes heavenly influence to produce outward manifestations on your behalf.

Validation Power of God's Will

So, again when we don't operate the Kingdom of God's way, we lose the power of validation in our situations and in our own hearts. Like Elijah, there is a bold confidence that comes from knowing we've connected to God's heart about the matter, and by connecting to His prosperous plan, favorable outcomes are inevitable.

I love what Jesus says concerning the validation principle in John 8:14:

> *Whereupon the Pharisees told Him, You are testifying on Your own behalf; Your testimony is not valid and is worthless. Jesus answered...My testimony is true and reliable and valid, for I know where I came from and where I am going.*

Here, the Pharisees are trying to discredit the covenant power of Jesus' words by accusing Him of testifying on His own behalf. Remember that *testimony* in Greek refers to covenant power. You see, everything Jesus is saying requires agreement in order for it to be a tangible truth for those who hear it. The Pharisees are a lot like the enemy who uses accusation after accusation of self-validation to discredit the power of our words. In other words, when we pray in self-effort or self-testimony, our authority is not validated because we are praying words of our own power.

This is a spiritual law in operation. Many times the enemy is able to confuse our situation further and even sometimes block our prayers because the validity of self-effort praying is illegal in the Kingdom of God. Our word power gains its strength from sure agreement with God's sound in the earth.

When we change positions in our prayer paradigm to listening and receiving from God, we legally charge heaven's atmosphere to break forth without limits because now we have not testified on our own. We have leveraged the contract power of words through agreement with God and His sound, enforcing into the earth realm what He has already been saying about us. So notice one of Jesus' main responses to the Pharisee's criticism of His words:

So Jesus added, When you have lifted up the Son of Man [on the cross], you will realize (know, understand) that I am He [for Whom you look] and that I do nothing of Myself (of My own accord or on My own authority), but I say [exactly] what My Father has taught Me.

John 8:28 (AMP)

You see, when we abort the validation power of a joint partnership with God in prayer, there is a hurling accusation being thrown at us in the shadows of spiritual realm. That accusation is that our words and petitions are not valid because they have flown from our own will rather than the will of God. Though people may not realize they self-validate with prayer a lot, by trying to get God to do things our way, in our time and solely what we want leaves no room for Him to ever reveal to us His heart about the matter. Instead, our approach should be a receiving one, genuinely desiring God's will about the situation.

This becomes easier the more we realize that God's will is predestined to prosper us and not harm us. We can trust that He has good things in store for us. As we lay down our own perspective and self-imposed motives concerning prayer, God will infuse our words with supercharged petitions that flow directly from His throne. There will be no limits as we join with Him concerning His prosperous plan for increasing mankind and our own personal lives.

Here our validation power takes flight, authorizing our rights as divine beings to do incredible things in the earth through the power of prayer. We can enforce heaven legally without constraint as we adopt the same principles as Jesus: *As we lift Him up, and value His will over ours, we will see that He is all that He claims to be and can do all that He promises.* Never again will your prayers go unheard or will your requests be denied. For nothing you say will be of your own accord or authority; rather it will be infused with the unlimited and sovereign power of God's will. He'll be using your words to supersede the kingdoms of this world.

This empowers you to rise above every accusation and fearful thought that somehow your words will not be heard and your prayers will not be answered. When negative thoughts try to discourage you of this, understand that God's validation of you empowers you to respond back: *"I don't agree with you and I know that my prayers have been answered, for I have not spoken on my own authority but based on the will of God."*

Keep decreeing this with boldness and confidence and watch those negative thoughts flee as the power of agreement with God's language system positions you to release unlimited word power in your life for supernatural manifestations. It's your time for unlimited power!

Empowering Thoughts, Empowered Words

We have favor; there is no doubt about that. However, our language must follow the pattern of a psychological state influenced by the reality of the Blessing. That Blessing is powerful enough to produce circumstances that can lead us into our next season of opportunity and simultaneous breakthrough.

When we focus on this state of favor rather than the conditions of our present circumstances, we are more likely to remain conscious of God's presence in us. We must focus on channeling His empowered will through words. We must hold to the empowered language of Blessing and God's will. We must hold to our internal state of favor and increase.

We are co-heirs with Christ and seeds of Abraham. That makes us legal beneficiaries of God's promise to the Abrahamic covenant. The promise is the Blessing and it is designed to draw wealth in our lives and to wipe out every trace of sorrow. Sure, that doesn't happen immediately on the outside, but you can be sure that beyond the surface of things the Blessing of God leverages the signature ink of your tongue to put into perpetuation some dynamic manifestations on your behalf.

If we can wipe out sorrow from our tongues through thoughts empowered by the Blessing, our prayers will become the pathway for a harvest of favor. When we feel the desire to repeat ourselves continually or to slip back into a lengthy self-effort style of praying, we must challenge those thoughts with the picture of rest in our redeemed spirit. We have to remember God validates our prayers, not us.

We don't speak of our own, but our authority flows from the Kingdom of God, which manifests itself as a tangible expression of God's will operating in our lives. This is how our words become spiritual contracts of grace and divine influence; when the sources of our thoughts become powered with God's heart as we internally evolve into the powerful unlimited beings that exist in our spirit.

The empowering language of Blessing is about to empower your life as you lead with God's will and not yours. You are authorized, validated and destined to be a living manifestation of God's greatness through your empowered language of confident and bold expectation for the Blessing to show up and overtake you.

Power Concepts from this Chapter

❖ We have been translated into the Kingdom of God, and our language system controls how much of the Kingdom system actually shows up in our life.

❖ It's easy to tell what country people are from by their native language. Language reveals the culture and nation prevalent in a person's life.

❖ Babbling is the mark of a person whose accent and language are still being influenced by a kingdom and culture that is outside of God's Blessing.

❖ When you pray correctly by making God's sound, God shows up, not the devil.

❖ When we take prayer out of its original design and Kingdom context, we become accustomed to traditions and form habits that God didn't teach us.

❖ Prayer was designed for us to receive from God a genuine download as we listen to His heart and clearly communicate that sound in the earth realm for manifestation.

❖ A wise heart, one that is governed by the principles of God's Word, is more likely to receive instruction rather than produce wordiness that is uninspired by God.

12 Ways to Operate the Kingdom Laws of Prayer

11

The Law of Petition

Now, again I want to encourage you that prayer is truly designed for you to receive whatever you ask for as Jesus promised. The reason Jesus promised it is because He wants that understanding and perspective of boldness to inspire our belief systems and expectations concerning prayer. He wants to be held to His promise that He will do what we ask. Again, by asking in this sense I mean petition.

The most known way to operate the law of prayer is by asking God through petitions and supplications. I want you to notice, though, that when Jesus tells us to ask, He says, *"Ask in prayer."* What I am about to point out may seem like a tiny detail, but I am telling you that this principle will amplify your prayer life greatly.

By telling us to ask in prayer, Jesus strategically makes distinction between *asking* and *prayer*. He makes it clear that asking is operated in prayer, but that the two are not the same function. You see, as I have been saying all along, prayer is the language system of heaven that attracts good things into our lives. Our desires are what we ask for; however, these desires have to conform to God's contingency plan.

In other words, when we ask for things that are not completely aligned with God's perfect pleasure He will teach us how to conform our words to match what He is thinking.

If we don't listen after we have asked then we abort the most important part of the process. God doesn't necessarily inform you but He will always conform you. Look at this scripture verse in Romans 8:29:

> *For those God foreknew he also predestined to be conformed to the image of his Son, that he might be the firstborn among many brothers and sisters.*

God conforms us into His image or pattern. This means a major part of our experience as citizens in His Kingdom is accompanied by the principle of conformation. What we ask for isn't always what needs to be asked for; sometimes our prayers need to be adjusted and so God has to *conform* us.

Again earth was created for man, the human kingdom. Romans 8 reminds us at that the same creation is waiting for the sons of God to show up and operate in their true authority. That's you and me.

If earth was created for the human kingdom then it's designed to respond to our desires. We just have to remember to concentrate on our divine right to influence this earth with our divine ability.

Gain a clear picture of what you desire. Take it to God and allow His thoughts to conform it to His desire. Then release a faith-filled request according to God's will to manifest your desire. It will be done for you; believe you have received and keep that picture in your mind.

If you remain in me and my words remain in you, ask whatever you wish, and it will be done for you.

John 15:7

The Law of Contracts: The Hannah Model

Remember that God is a contractor trying to win the bidding war for your tongue. This is one of the dimensions of God's mind: making contracts. Sometimes what we desire from God isn't going to be answered simply through asking or declarations. Some things require a clear form of agreement between you and the Creator to manifest your desires along with something He wants to do through you in the earth.

I like to draw from the example of Hannah. She struggled for years to get her prayer answered concerning having a child. Every year she would go up to offer sacrifices and pray eagerly for a child. However, she got the same results every time. Finally, Hannah got a download from God and she changed language systems. This opened the door to a new communication route and opportunity for heaven to intervene.

She made a contract with God to give her son as priest to the House of God if He would bless her. That same day she became pregnant. See, God was going to need a priest 15 years later. Well, when Hannah contracted God's desire by connecting her will to His, the laws of prayer were correctly operated and He "heard" her prayer and released manifestation that same day. There may be something you need turnaround in but it seems to linger on. Try seeking God's heart concerning His purpose through you and make a legal binding agreement with Him to honor that purpose through your answered prayer.

And she made a vow (contract), saying, "Lord Almighty, if you will only look on your servant's misery and remember me, and not forget your servant but give her a son, then I will give him to the Lord for all the days of his life, and no razor will ever be used on his head."

1 Samuel 1:11 [Parenthesis added by author]

The Law of Remembrance

One thing we need to always hold in our hearts about God is that He is the God of covenant blessing. He honors His covenant with whomever He's made it for generations after they have died.

This can benefit us in many ways, especially when it comes to making petitions to the Lord. We are indeed covenant beneficiaries of the Abrahamic policy. However, we have to understand that the Blessing of Abraham came through Abraham and not us. For this reason we need to be skillful and consistent about reminding God who He made His covenant with. To *remember* in the Hebrew sense is much different than the westernized perspective of this word. When God "remembers" He holds Himself accountable to a specific promise or blessing He performed. This means He sees you as the same as that person, blessing you in the same manner. This is what many of the Old Testament characters were seeking when they called on God to "remember them." They were calling His attention to a specific time and blessing He had performed.

In the same way, the remembrance policy is a powerful principle to answered prayer. We can find covenants in the Bible, build our faith in them, and call God to remembrance concerning His policy. This especially works with the New Testament policy of blessing. Jesus tells us that bread and wine are representational of a new covenant policy He is instituting. That fulfillment is only found in the Kingdom of God now, and that is how we are to dine and commune with Him.

He said, "as often as you do this, you call me to *remembrance*." What is this policy? When we function according to the stipulations of this covenant of faith in the blood, we call Jesus to remembrance of every promise holding Him accountable to every covenant blessing both spiritual and material through our obedience.

This law of remembrance is still at work. Grab ahold to God's promises, call Him to remembrance and ask Him not to see you but the person He did it for. In this way, by faith you become an heir to that blessing and possessor of that promise.

> *In the same manner he also took the cup after supper saying, "This cup is the new covenant in my blood this do as often as you do in remembrance of me."*

> 1 Corinthians 11:25 (NKJV)

The Law of Decreeing

Decreeing is a powerful Kingdom principle concerning prayer. In this dynamic form of bold praying we adhere to what God has said and leverage its influence to create powerful statements of faith over situations and our lives. In the simplest of terms, to decree is to establish policy; this is the operation of kings. Now remember, the earth is our kingdom and it is designed to respond to the human, its ruler.

When you decree something, you are establishing Kingdom policy that is to govern in your life as you command. You can perform decrees in the form of daily affirmations to coach the right mindset and state of mind that will draw and attract Blessing. However, a decree over a situation is not to be repeated over and over, as when a king establishes law he does not have to repeat himself. This is a powerful form of prayer.

A perfect example of this is Jesus at the fig tree with His disciples. Jesus was confident in the laws of decreeing. He simply approached the tree and stated His demands. Then He left. The next day the tree was uprooted as He had commanded it. What's interesting is He told the disciples if they tap into faith they could do this with a mountain! In other words He was saying, *"Forget about the fig tree; if you tap into this principle it has to work with a mountain."*

Notice how Jesus never repeated Himself after speaking to the tree. And the most important part: He walked away. Why did Jesus do this even though He didn't see any results from what He said?

Jesus was able to walk away because He knew the law of faith was already functioning on its own. He didn't stay to see what would happen because He had already received it by faith, and He understood the law of decreeing is a set invariable principle holding to the same results when used properly. You must tap into the kingship paradigm to exercise this authoritative stance of prayer. Psychologically you must not entertain the possibility of another outcome other than what you have said.

You are the policy enforcer of heaven. Gain a clear picture of God's expected outcome from you through His Word. Tune your words accordingly and make bold decrees based on the promises of God. In the face of adversity, remember your decree and say back to yourself: *My words are government policy; therefore, my favorable and winning outcome is sure to come to pass.*

When you charge your life with the power of decreeing, you are setting yourself up for unstoppable victory. Policy dictates the outcome and your decree positions you to look forward to Kingdom policy that can't be undone or overturned. Decree over your life, finances, and relationships. Stay in agreement with them and watch your world conform to the government policy of God's favor and increase.

And you will decree a thing and it will be established.

Job 22:28

The Law of Confession

Confession in the Greek means to say what has already been said. The key point here is agreement with something that has been said. So, what is God saying about you? It's your job to find out in His Word and copy His sound. In prayer, listen, wait to receive from God because He is always thinking and saying something about your life.

When you adjust to God's voice you can repeat that same sound in the form of daily confession that mirrors God's will for your life. Everyday you can make new confessions to inspire good thoughts about you and your expectations. You can reaffirm to yourself who you are and what you are capable of. You can rule your day by owning the morning with words of life, peace, and prosperity. Just agree with God.

You have to decide and determine that no matter what, I am not going to agree with what my eyes see, I am going to agree with God. If God says you're debt free well then just agree with Him, not the bank. If God says you're healed then just agree with Him, not sickness.

The difference between the law of confession and decreeing is again, decrees are generally not to be repeated; they are one-time policy declarations that establish God's will as policy in your life. However, confessions can be operated daily to encourage thought patterns that align with your decree. Your daily confession is your declaration of who and what gets access and entry into your life. I encourage you to get my prayer books along with this one and learn to make your confession and reflection of God's prosperous thoughts toward you.

By doing this you are creating a continual flow of heaven's sound channeling God's life through your words. Be confident, bold and aware of your present position as a royal citizen in the Kingdom of God.

Remember that confession is a law and is always working for you, not through effort but by grace through your faith. Make your confession everyday, establish this habit and determine in your heart not to waver from it no matter what circumstances arise to contradict your words.

> *For it is with your heart that you believe and are justified, and it is with your mouth that confession is made and you are saved.*

Romans 10:10

The Law of Celebration

Take into account this statement: Continual praise perpetuates an atmosphere of expectation, which is the breeding ground for miracles. Did you know that praise is a strategic form of prayer designed to incline God's ear to your words? Praise and celebration are forms of thanksgiving to God. When we celebrate we learn not to cut off our faith at what God has done but to perpetually believe Him for more.

Creating expectation is only possible when we create the right chemical state in our minds of perceived positive outcome by infusing our emotions, bodies, and words with celebration of victory. See, many individuals who have won will chant victory chants. Well, it should be no different for you. You are victorious, you are a winner, now make the sound of champions. Praise releases energy of a champion and victor so that is what you attract, the life of a victor.

Celebration also indicates gratitude, which has been confirmed through recent studies to have extremely positive impact on the body and brain. Praise God with thanksgiving and create positive thought patterns that will produce rest, especially in challenging seasons. What you are willing to praise God for now will become a down payment on the breakthrough that's coming in your life. Sometimes our answer isn't a decree or supplication, rather in a joyful noise unto God.

Just as Paul and Silas prayed in prison and released the sound of heaven to break through, so can your praise produce an atmosphere of incredible miracles and cataclysmic happenings. Leverage the spirit of thanksgiving and praise to celebrate your way into the miraculous and supernatural.

Let the message of Christ dwell among you richly as you teach and admonish one another with all wisdom through psalms, hymns, and songs from the Spirit, singing to God with gratitude in your hearts.

Colossians 3:16

The Law of Meditation

Prayer cannot be operated effectively outside of a spiritual and psychological state in which one has full agreement with their inner-self. With that said, one of the hidden art forms of the Bible is the power of meditation. This hidden art form of prayer teaches us to inscribe the Word of God within the subconscious of our being. Although we are not aware of it, our subconscious thoughts are responsible for much of the operation of our body. The power of our subconscious can have the same lasting effect on our prayers if we will paint the right pictures of God's Word for it to function on its own.

When we meditate on God's words we are tuning our hearts to line up with the sound of heaven. We are repelling negative thoughts that become barriers and hindrances when trying to believe God for seemingly large requests in prayer. When we have laid the groundwork with meditation, our subconscious response to faith-filled requests will become pictures that align with what we are believing for.

Our subconscious is created to take in information, not give it out. It is subject to the thoughts we feed it. Remember that *word* in Greek is logos, which means thought or reason. When we meditate on the Word consistently we are charging our thoughts with God's very motive and intent. We are teaching our hearts to long after what is on God's mind.

This is why God taught Joshua to *meditate on His Word day and night*. Joshua was about to perform an amazing miracle and he needed to paint the right pictures in his mind. Before you pray, sometimes it's good to grab the scripture verses that agree with your desire and think on them in a silent place until you become totally immersed in the idea of that very thing happening according to the Word.

This process will infuse your thoughts and your words to speak only what God says and concentrate on the picture His words have painted on the canvas of your heart. Through meditation we hear from God and remove distractions. We concentrate more on the sound of heaven as the outside voices get quieter and God's internal audible voice within gets louder and louder. No matter what, don't allow the noisiness of life to drown out God's voice. Meditate on His Word. Silently repeat the Word and as you meditate just picture your desire being met and align with it. Allow it to build your confidence, and at your highest point of faith, say what you see in your thoughts and give it permission to exist externally. Meditation will take you to a new level of releasing a stream of perfect thoughts that flow directly from God's heart to yours.

God will write on your heart the right pictures, visions, and dreams to give you clarity of His prosperous will for every area of your life.

> *Keep this Book of the Law always on your lips; meditate on it day and night, so that you may be careful to do everything written in it. Then you will be prosperous and successful.*

Joshua 1:8

The Law of Wisdom & Instruction

One of the most powerful ways to leverage prayer is by asking God for sound wisdom and instruction. Many times we can become so tied to seeing our prayer manifested that we lose sight in the value of receiving sound instruction that can lead us to our manifestation.

In fact, we should be very cognizant of the fact that when we pray God is most likely going to reveal an instruction to us to follow. That is why listening is so important and the 1st principle of accurate praying. The Bible reminds us that wisdom is the principle thing. When frustration breaks out make it part of your success plan to immediately release faith to receive divine wisdom and instruction from God.

In the midst of chaos, God will slip us instruction that will turn the winds of adversity into winds of favor. To operate in this law of instruction we have to be determined not to allow what is going on around us to deter us from listening intently for God to speak.

Throughout the Bible there is account after account of God speaking to His servant with instruction on how to operate His Kingdom. He gave clear and concise instruction to Moses on how to free the children of Israel. He gave skilled and concise wisdom on how to construct the priest garment and how to build His temple. God is an instructor and He loves nothing more than to instruct us on how to receive from Him what we ask. Seeking wisdom is seeking God's heart, His Blessing, and plan.

I can recall a time when I was praying about finances and seeking God's wisdom to increase my financial situation. Later that week I went to sleep and had a dream of a particular stock of company that God was telling me to buy. When I woke up I went to my laptop to begin looking up this stock and seeing how it was trending.

Now, I didn't know a thing about stock markets or how to purchase stock. So, after a while I went to bed and a week later I received the same instruction. Again I looked up the stock but it was continuing in a devastating downward trend and all the reports on this stock said to leave it alone and not to buy it. However, I was not operating in emotion because prayer is a divine law that governs the spirit. So, I took some time learning how to purchase stock, set up an account, and waited for money to buy it.

Next, God gave me the name of people to tell about what He had said. I explained to them that even though this stock was in the red God assured me to buy it now and that it would triple within the next six months. They all believed me and we put our monies together to purchase as much available stock as possible.

Sure enough, within days that stock began to rise. In weeks it became a stock to watch. And within a few months it was doubling. By the end of the year the stock had tripled and was now one of the most watched stocks in the market. I was able to use that money to receive financial breakthrough in a season where I really needed it.

Our breakthrough lies in wisdom, and we have to believe and receive confidently that God is our source within and His life flow connects us to instruction that can lead us into positive outcomes.

> *If any of you lacks wisdom, you should ask God, who gives generously to all without finding fault, and it will be given to you. But when you ask, you must believe and not doubt.*

James 1:5-6

The Law of Sowing

Did you know that your words are seeds that will eventually bear the fruit of whatever you plant? The way this principle works as a law of prayer is by learning to plant seeds of greatness! What I am referring to is your understanding that prayer can release things but only with small beginnings. All big things have small beginnings, so it is with the expectation to produce major breakthrough with prayer.

In Matthew 13, Jesus describes this process of planting spiritual seed and reveals that whoever learns to sow the Word of God correctly will reap an abundant harvest with it. Now, you have to realize that the very antithesis of being a sower implies skill and intention. However, planting seed in God's Kingdom is not the same as what many are used to.

You see, in the Kingdom God, the sower learns to "scatter seed." This is an important principle when praying big things into the earth and an effective prayer strategy as well. In other words, you don't have to wait until one process is done in your life to begin believing God for something else. Plant the seed and move on.

You are a spiritual farmer in the Kingdom of God with a bag full of powerful seeds called the Bible. It provides all types of seed to produce any type of harvest you desire to see. You may believe God for great breakthrough in your finances but you also have some big requests in your relationship sphere too. Don't stretch yourself trying to believe God for a bunch of things in one season, but simply grab the Word of God that matches your need or desire. Agree with it and plant the seed by faith, speaking over that situation, and settle it with your faith that it is done. Keep doing this with any thing or any sphere of your life that you need to get results in. I am telling you, this principle of seeding with prayer is going to set you up for season after season of tangible release.

When you approach prayer with a seedtime harvest mentality, you can easily wipe out doubt and fear that usually try to accompany big requests. Many times our carnal mind will contradict our faith and make us think we are limited to a number or size of requests we can believe God for.

There are no limits; you are a royal son and joint heir of the Kingdom with Jesus Christ. Ask and receive, keep believing, and keep sowing seed with faith in God's Word.

You don't have to limit your requests, but you need to be sure of what you are focusing on in the right season. There is a time to sow and a time to reap. Leverage this law of sowing and reaping by scattering seed in your life financially, emotionally, and relationally. Make sure you settle it inside with your faith that the seed is good and that divine laws of seedtime and harvest are working for you. Go ahead and back that seed faith prayer up with financial seed faith. Now your faith is really working for you! Write down what you prayed for and sowed for and keep it somewhere you can always go back and check on it.

When contradictions show up, go back to your seed and look at it and remind your circumstances that the seed has already been planted. Shout over the seed in expectation of total victory. You'll soon notice that prayers are being answered left and right and a continual flow of increase and prosperity is taking over your life. Well, the more you sow the more you reap. Remember that he who sows much reaps much, but he who sows little will reap little.

There are no limits on this principle of scattering seed.

Trust that God is faithful to His promise and divine law system. He is watching over His Word (seed) to be sure that it is accomplished. Set yourself up for continuous breakthrough by approaching prayer with a seed faith paradigm.

> *Whoever sows sparingly will also reap sparingly, and whoever sows generously will also reap generously.*

2 Corinthians 9:6

The Law of Reaping

It's very important to understand that the law of sowing and the law of reaping are two separate functions although they are often mentioned together. Both require action in order to produce results. When reaping a harvest you have to visualize it coming and pray simple prayers of wisdom concerning your ability to "realize" a harvest when it shows up. In fact, the word *reap* in Hebrew comes from the word "realize." This is making the spiritual law of reaping work for you.

The Kingdom laws of reaping are actually tied to your focus and ability to know what God is doing in the right season and what to expect for that season too. If you aren't aware of what doors are open and what God is doing you will miss out on sound opportunities that may delay that Blessing from showing up for another season or two. If you can remember that in Numbers 13 the children of Israel, despite their miraculous experiences with God, could not believe God for the open door to possess the promise. They weren't aware of their reaping season, although God made it clear they were in one.

They missed the door and ended up dying without seeing the promise fulfilled. Remember this, if you aren't aware of doors that are open you could be potentially self-sabotaging your blessings.

Be consistent in always checking in with the Father about the season you are in and continually praying for revelation knowledge of the doors that are open to you in the right season. God will honor your faith and you will begin to "realize" what doors are open to you, waiting to bless you as soon as you walk through them.

This is how the law of reaping works. Ask, receive, and believe God for wisdom of how your answer will show up. Stay focused on that harvest, thank God for it, and watch closely for opportunities that may present themselves in glimpses. I don't care how small the door may seem to be, speak up, make yourself known and walk through it. Sometimes you have to let people know who you are and what you're believing for or you'll miss your door to reap blessing.

Doors in the Kingdom do not open like doors we see everyday. They are usually like those motion sensor sliding doors: the closer you get to the right place you will trigger a spiritual motion detector and the door will open for you. However, just like most sliding doors, that spiritual door will close as quickly as it opened.

It's up to you whether it closes in front of you or behind you. In the same way Jesus reminds us the gates (doors) that lead to destruction are broad and the gates that lead to life (life in the Kingdom) are narrow. I cannot tell you how many times we pray for something major and walk right outside and the door slides open, but we overlook it and it closes right in front of us. Getting results with the law of reaping demands that you understand heaven is a spiritual place which functions by what I call the *open door policy*. God will grant us whatever we want but we have to recognize where the door is open, walk through and possess the harvest.

Again, sometimes you have to squeeze into the door that God presents. But be sure He is faithful to these laws of prayer. If we speak His language right He will respond, and many times doors open faster than we realize. Other times you have to be patient, trusting in the seed you've sown, skillfully waiting for the right time to reap your harvest.

When you are really working the reaping principle, you will trigger the right movement and walk through the right opportunity to reap tangible manifestation of faith seeds you've been sowing.

The Law of Forgiveness

Our prayers are spiritual; they are intrinsic and flow from the inner most of our being. They flow from faith, and faith finds its foundation in love. In fact, faith works by love, because love is simply favor, unmerited kindness and pure intention.

Did you know that we have the ability to block our prayers? That is what happens when we harbor unforgiveness. Believe it or not many times people don't get their manifestation of praying simply because they have failed to truly forgive and release someone who's done them wrong.

Jesus is clear that grace is given and flows through our faith in Him. Our faith is a direct proponent of God's love. If we aren't forgiving others then we have disconnected from love and from true faith that births miracles and manifestations. I will tell you that if you want to see more prayers answered, concentrate on operating in love more.

When we forgive, we release what I call spiritual debt. When we have spiritual debt we are bankrupt on faith and love. We don't have spiritual currency to make powerful transactions with our prayers. If you will open your heart to this principle you will notice that God will begin to show you names of people you haven't forgiven. He will show you how to unblock certain prayers by releasing hurts and unforgiveness.

In my own personal life, I've watched as God will continually show me people I have not forgiven for certain things. It's not my intention, and neither is it yours, but our hearts have a way of clinging to the past. We have to apply faith and humility to move beyond the pain into loving them again. Here the perfect picture of God's purpose is manifested.

This doesn't mean God won't answer any of your prayers, but there are some prayers He will not answer to push you into the direction of love and obedience by granting pardons to people who have hurt us. We have to make this principle a constant habit and be sure to examine closely a thought we have towards anyone.

When you sow a release of forgiveness, you reap a release of answered prayer. This could be a barrier to something you've asked for and didn't get. It's so valuable and near to God's heart that we seek Him to learn when our heart is aligned with His. You'll see the difference when you pray with forgiveness versus with unforgiveness residing in your heart. It will change your life, free your heart, and increase your faith as you are tapping into real love, real favor, and great expectation.

> *If you forgive other people when they sin against you, your heavenly Father will also forgive you.*

Matthew 6:14

The Law of Love
Break up with fear

Love is the language of heaven. God only speaks to us in love and fills our thoughts with His favor toward us. You have to kick out any thought that riots against those ideas of love and security.

Not understanding God's love for you will hinder your faith and ability to rise above slavish fear trying to convince you that God isn't going to come through. Don't entertain that fear; look at love.

Slavish fear is always present in the heart where there is no true knowledge of sonship. Romans 8:15, shares a powerful principle concerning sonship:

> *The Spirit you received does not make you slaves, so that you live in fear again; rather, the Spirit you received brought about your adoption to sonship.*

The spirit of fear makes our petitions vulnerable to doubt and many times it seems the moment we ask in faith, doubt fills our hearts with thoughts of that prayer not manifesting. This is called slavish fear and you have to combat it by concentrating your thoughts on God's love.

You can win against every accusation of doubt and fear by speaking the truth about how much God loves you, that you are His son, and the Kingdom is your inheritance to reap the fruit of answered prayer. Fear will cause you to think on things that you don't want to come to pass. Remember your subconscious thoughts attract the pictures you concentrate on in your life. Subject your thought's to scriptures that remind you of the favor you have in Christ and in His Kingdom.

Having God's love means you have the King's approval. It means you are sealed with victory and God has endorsed your life. Leverage this God-endorsement to make bold requests free from doubt that break the limitations off of your life. Believe God and rely on your constant acknowledgement of His love and favor to bring you into unstoppable faith.

Live in Love

Do nice things for others that you would like to see done in your life. God will often times give us the opportunity to meet the same need we have in someone else's life on a lower level. We should literally be looking for opportunity to help meet someone else's needs, that way no need that shows up in our life can stick around for long.

When we walk in love we are accountable to what moves God, not just us. Remember that prayer is not a self-effort; it is a form of acknowledgement concerning God's heart for man. Many people are asking, "God, why aren't you answering my prayer?" God is saying back to them, "Why aren't you walking in love?" Always look for chances to give.

You can live by how you give. Don't just use prayer for yourself, constantly plant seeds of greatness in others. Always speak life into what other people are doing. Stay away from gossip and pointing out negativity in someone else's life. All of these create the wrong sound waves and produce inconsistency in our heavenly language of life and love.

The more we walk in love the more we will walk in faith. And I'm telling you the Kingdom of God will become more of a conscious reality as God continually express His heart to us through our communication and life of giving and unmerited kindness. Bless those who curse you, pray for your enemies because you are literally setting yourself up to reap blessing after blessing by communicating in love.

Gain the Right Motive

No matter how much we love God it's possible for us at any time to pray outside of God's motives for our life. This means we sometimes can be driven by factors outside of the Master's plan and where He is trying to take us. Now remember, in the Kingdom you are willingly submitting to the will of the King. This means how you operate, especially in prayer, must be centered on what God is thinking.

For this reason we have to be constantly filling our thoughts with words of life that direct us towards God's prosperous plan. We have to build faith and trust in God's plan over ours so that over time we are conscious of His ways, believing that He is always working for our best possible outcome. Make yourself reliant on His plan and receive your rest. When you know you're being empowered by God's plans and not your own, you can have confidence in your petitions to the Lord.

You make positive declarations knowing you are shaping a supportive paradigm that promotes God's will and not your own. Here the validity of prayer takes shape and you are able to rise above every accusation of negative forces by placing your trust in God's plan.

Be sure to declare regularly over yourself words of affirmation that remind you that God's will is the best plan for your life. Declare that His will is His promise and He is demonstrating that promise in you, through you, and for you in order to bring you into greater levels of living.

The Restoration of Divine Communication

The gift of communication has been restored through the Blessing connection of God's Kingdom. Our rights as Kingdom citizens emerge from the confidence in knowing that we are redeemed, born again, and positioned for unlimited favor as royal sons in God's family.

The entire platform of God's plan to send His son to reproduce sons in His family is built on God's desire and intent to return us to the original policy and plan of Eden where our communication is unlimited and unhindered with our divine source. Our prayers become channels of influence that express our redeemed position in God.

When we learn to view the language of prayer as a communing device to produce God's purpose of total fellowship with us, we tap into the power of His will and unleash the mysterious force that shaped creation.

Prayer is creative power. The secret to unleashing this

power lies in the constant communication we have with our Creator. We can literally attract blessings and increase and repel negative situations.

Prayer has the ability to intercept negative assignments forged against our lives to rob us of our inheritance and divine prosperity. When you access the laws of prayer and learn to apply them accurately, no force will be able to stop you. A prayer paradigm is empowered by the belief system that "I am" exists internally and we can draw from our source to produce breakthrough at any time.

The endless stream of God's thoughts are readily accessible to us to release strategy, truth, wisdom and understanding that will materialize any supplication regardless of how big it may seem. Prayer is law that works every time when the right pattern is followed for producing results.

You have to empower your psychological state with ideas that flow from the goodness of God's love and the Blessing on your life. Remain consciously aware that the more you agree with your redeemed state of royal heirship, the more the Kingdom comes alive in you. You will access the place to rule from as God inspires and leads from the governing seat of your heart. Prayer is a divine form of ruling power.

Our approach to the Kingdom of God has to be renewed and empowered with a now and complete perspective of life. Our current state as members of God's royal congress (body) is a winning position.

Winners don't pray from a defeated end. The champion within you is not communicating a sorrowful laborious style of praying. You have to agree in your heart with the picture of the undefeated you and disconnect from anything that riots against your perfected state.

You don't have to feel perfected; however, "by His stripes you are made whole." When we arrive at the completed state of thought, we tap into a winner's paradigm and our chances of living in total victory are increased with every positive thought, word, and declaration of truth.

You see, when we tap into truth we access higher living. Truth is the highest reality that conforms previously spoken things to the image of the Son. God's pattern of breakthrough is powered by our desire to live in truth no matter how it may contradict common reasoning. Functioning the law of prayer is a total commitment to no longer view your circumstances through the five senses but to perceive by faith in the Kingdom of God and His way of doing things.

This is where boldness kicks in. Our bold approach will develop within us the confidence needed to withstand negative forecasts and fearful signs of the future. We don't have to agree with any outcome that doesn't line up with God's victorious Blessing and plan. Confidence is our pillar of faith that keeps us accountable to the Kingdom way of life.

We have to be bold enough to stand in the face of fear and declare that we are not backing down, we are standing on favor and that we possess the royal right to manifest every promise in God's Word. In this sense we are "manifesting the sons of God" because we are operating in our complete nature, boldly approaching the throne of grace and supplicating on our behalf in confidence of our redemption.

That confidence should carry on into every realm of our life, including how we speak to all things. We can come boldly to God's throne asking and receiving when our sound waves connect with His frequency. The question we have to always be asking ourselves is "are we making the sound of life or the sound of death?" It's amazing how much you'll notice we say throughout the day that doesn't line up with the Kingdom language of life and blessing.

This seemingly small factor is at the root of many

unanswered prayers as we have failed to streamline God's sound correctly by allowing traces of the Babylonian kingdom to fill our airwaves. Of course, we are under grace and possess the ability to tap back into divine communication by humbling ourselves and disconnecting from negative sources, forces, and influences.

Coming to terms with this principle of sound means we also come to terms with the reality that it's possible to pray wrong. God doesn't hear every prayer and we cannot let this offend us. We have to understand that laws are invariable, fixed rules that are unchanging, producing the same results under the same conditions.

If we don't function the laws of prayer correctly we will experience interruptions and frustrations. However, we are in a place of total communion with God, as we will ask Him to teach us how to pray. The disciples tapped into this in Matthew 6 and by asking they received the secret attracting to us any desire we have through Kingdom laws of communication. We can possess that same system by asking.

So again, law is functioning all the time every day and all around us. Force perpetuates these laws and creates continual results. We have to view sound, language, and words as laws governing the system of life.

Creation is based on the law of sound. God spoke His Word, or sound, for six days producing from the invisible into the seen realm all we are able to witness in creation today. That means the universal law of sound is built into creation constantly governing our affairs when we speak. With that said, our sound is life or death, blessing or curse, prosperity or lack.

Our tongues give contractual permission for things to manifest in our lives and we have the signature power of ink through our words. What we say all the time is an invitation for those very things to show up.

One simple change in our way of thinking can open the door to a new way of living and receiving from God. Use the principles in this book to guide you into the accurate protocol of prayer. Leverage wisdom as a helpful resource to understand more clearly the power of language.

Your problems are not as big as they seem and there is a contract in heaven with your name on it guaranteed to produce the things you want in life. When you learn to partner with God through His will, you learn to communicate that will as powerful life-charging atoms fill your atmosphere with particles of blessings. You can expect a release from the positive charges of praying heaven's will into your atmosphere.

In this way, testimony, confession, and decrees will always be valid because your authority isn't of your own; you're validated by the conversation God is having with you in your heart. That's where your positive confession flows from: thoughts empowered by your God nature.

God is thinking great things about you. Are you? You can leverage prayer to tap into that positive stream of life-giving concepts that will eventually influence your words as expressions of God's energy. God's life is in you and He's waiting to express Himself through bold acts of faith and courageous petitions that take the limits off of what He can do.

There are no limits to your asking. What is it that you desire? Do you know? Are you really concentrating on the full picture when you pray for it? Learn to meditate and guide your thoughts into a clear projection of what you want to attract and desire to see happen in your life.

By doing this, you are powering your subconscious state, creating a greater realization of heaven's open door policy that's waiting to unleash tangible opportunities for you to reap your harvest. Your lifeline in prayer is conscious agreement with God's favor and your present position as a son or daughter. Don't let go of who you are. Don't be intimidated by outside circumstances that contradict what you've believed for.

No matter what, stand on the solid foundation of the God in you. Know that you have access to unlimited wisdom that will teach you how to reap your harvest.

God will guide your words, lead your footsteps, and create the pathways that will accelerate your breakthrough. You will learn to thrive with prayer and become a skillful communicator of life and the empowered language of the Blessing. Remember to speak life to all things, to all people, at all times. Avoid wordiness and stand on the confident and bold mindset that you're in covenant with the King and it has no expiration date. Tell God He has total rights to the bidding war for your tongue.

It's time to eradicate all frustration of inconsistent living and unanswered prayer. Know that God is faithful to His policy to meet every need and enforce Blessing and prosperity into your life. There is a way to ensure that God hears every prayer and your requests are never denied. There is a way to overcome the constant accusation of slavish fear and abandonment. This is your season to reap the harvest of seed you've sown without the understanding of how to reap.

Prepare for real influence. Position and posture your heart to eliminate the gaps of unfulfilled requests. You are a divine diplomat in the earth operating on heaven's behalf and communicating God's will as a joint-effort rather than a self-effort. God's divine plan of diplomacy is your source for provision. You are empowered by God's royal intent of Kingdom deployment. Release faith and prepare your heart to become a pathway of unstoppable increase and a tangible channel of God's favor.

From now on when you ask you will receive. You will declare things and they will show up. You will decree anything and it's going to be established by your words. Allow the powerful force of high impact prayer to empower your life just as the patriarchs of the Bible. This is your Elijah moment and your Esther breakthrough. You have been brought into the Kingdom for such a time as this. As it is in heaven let it be in the earth, the divine power of enforcing God's will. God's grace is with you, strengthening your every word with life, intention, love, and empowering sounds. Amen.

Power Concepts from this Chapter

❖ When you pray for something, you have to recognize where the door is open, walk through, and possess the harvest.

❖ When you sow a release of forgiveness, you reap a release of answered prayer.

❖ When a need shows up in your life, don't pass the opportunity to meet someone else's need on a lower level.

❖ When you decree something, do not entertain the possibility of another outcome other than what you have said.

❖ Don't allow traces of the Babylonian kingdom to fill your airwaves; always be conscious of lining up with the Kingdom language of life and blessing.

❖ Every sound we make is life or death, blessing or curse, prosperity or lack.

Made in the USA
Charleston, SC
05 November 2014